Moral Orientation of the Senior Leadership In a Fortune 100 Corporation

By
Dr. Susan Harwood

Moral Orientation Leadership: a comparative study

First softcover printing 2013
Original hardcover publication 1996
Published by

www.walkerpublications.com

ISBN-13: 978-0988250819
Title ID: 4159441

Dedication
To
Dr. Carolyn Desjardins
1930 - 1997

There are people who enter our lives and leave a forever imprint expanding who we are and how we see the world just for having known them. This is the legacy that Dr. Carolyn Desjardins imparted into my life and the lives of hundreds of women whose life journeys she was a part. Carolyn was a renascence woman of wisdom, strength, compassion, humor, and intellect, sharing unconditional love. She was my mentor, my confidante, my colleague, and my friend.

She taught me how to research, to live each day to the fullest, to explore all of who I am, and in the end, she showed me how to move to the other side with dignity and anticipation.

With the utmost in respect and admiration...

........you are missed.....Susan

Essay: Were We Right??
By Dr. Susan Harwood

As I was preparing the 2nd edition release of my research in moral orientation and leadership, I kept asking three fundamental questions: "Were we right?"; "What did we miss?"; "What's next?". Did the findings in leader moral orientation, the increased number of "knowledge workers" in organizations, and the impact of the global marketplace remain relevant as reviewed in the literature section of the study?

These trends and the integration of the research fields of psychology, leadership, organization culture, and motivation being redefined in a global economy was a daunting task. The interrelationships of the four research fields explored in this study are as powerful today as they were when the study was originally conducted. The question of how large numbers of knowledge workers, investments in leadership development, and the changing dynamics within corporate cultures interplay with the moral orientation of the leaders responsible for guiding US corporations through the complex maze of global opportunities may be more relevant today.

Unfortunately, the progress in these areas has been slow if not regressive. How we saw the next steps in advancing and changing our organizations to keep pace with this dynamic global market, knowledge worker potential and leaders with Dual moral orientation have not yet been fully realized.

Knowledge worker expectations of work environments and leaders drove many of the progressive changes in collaborative decision-making, while investments in their learning inspired new technology, business models, and market creation. Businesses adopted distributed organization models that cross company and country boundaries. Production in China, design in the US and distribution channels by global regions are no longer a unique approach to successful profitability. It was a time of exciting pioneering.

Leaders created ever expanding visions. Investments in leadership and management development began creating leaders with dual moral orientation styles. Inclusion became a valuable tool for organizational alignment and the exploding internet options gave faster response platforms removing location barriers, enabling faster decision-making abilities.

The global economy was booming and we were driving along the road of unprecedented profits and technology. Then we hit the economic downturn wall which sent markets reeling and business scrambling.

Moral Orientation Leadership: a comparative study

What did we miss?

The impact the emerging China would have on global productivity as they "simultaneously implemented programs of liberalization, privatization, and marketization" (Lin 2010) moving quickly through the foundation stages of economic transformation. Linda Lim (1997) describes the power that emerges wwith one-third of the world's population residing in the East and Southeast Asia predicting the 21st century as the "Asian century".

Joshua Sanders (2010) outlines the lessons to be learned as Germany and China emerged as the "winners" in the economic downturn. The establishment of an international series of financial transaction maze creating inflated mortgages and inflated corporate worth. This is an economic sampling of what experts would identify as what we missed economically. These are some of the economic topics to be explored to gain a full understanding what drove many decisions in the first decade of the 21st century.

I will confine this essay to briefly exploring the "what we missed" topics related to the original leadership moral orientation study: Learning & Development; Innovation & Motivation; and Leaders & Corporate Culture.

Learning & Development

The original study was conducted during the expansive learning organization boom of the 1990's. As the economy changed, once again learning was viewed not as a competitive advantage, but a cost item. The result was a decade of minimal new employee education and a continual cycle of "more of the same".

The saying a duck is a duck no matter what you call it seems appropriate here. Shorter Cycle Times + Quality Improvements (be it quality teams, or sigma champions) = Productivity Improvements. This formula has been repackaged and tweaked many times since the Deming days, but the core set of expectations and solutions have been the same.

The mantra of *faster, cheaper, with higher quality* is the expected norm in the global competitive marketplace. However, there is a significant difference between basic fundamentals of success and breakthrough competitive advantage. These initiatives have been rearranged, renamed, and repacked but the underlying concepts have been the same since the 1980's.

Processes improvements do produce efficiencies; the question is how to invest dollars gained by implementing the new efficiencies. Investments in people development were eliminated in favor of increased profitability. In markets which were struggling to keep pace with new technology and products; the gains were used to shore up "same rate" profitability; the expectation of more profit, faster. Mintzberg's question (2007) "What does the phrase '*Lean and mean*' tell us about the times?", is an accurate reflection of the mutated path productivity programs led (and continue to lead) many corporations.

Organizations with this focus leave little room for creativity and innovation. Employees continually measured on standards will become standard experts, but will not concurrently try new ideas, experiment to learn, or innovate.

Moral Orientation Leadership: a comparative study

Our accounting systems place people in the cost column of the balance sheet and not the asset column reinforcing the idea that they are disposable. Productivity initiatives focused solely on optimizing the process and reducing the investments in the education and development of the people do not create learning cycles broad enough to address the global complexities of the 21st century. New employees who do not have the benefit of the learning of the 1990's struggle for context of the original intent of these productivity programs.

Dynamic learning systems which provided varied learning opportunities to accommodate the diverse learning styles of people have been repackaged with a large influx of "online learning solutions". Certainly online courses do provide a cost effective way to meet low level skill or compliance requirements. Even with the advancements in technology, most packaged online learning lacks the opportunity for live robust discussions, building relationship awareness, or accommodating the learning styles of the majority of the workforce.

The creativity and innovation which learning sparks is lost in the boundaries of the online platform and the boredom of the learner on the platform. A blended set of learning opportunities incorporating multiple learning approaches and self-directed learning options as described in the Guglielmino studies (1988) seem to have been abandoned in favor of faster, cheaper, standardization.

Even in the Fortune 100 Corporation in the original study, abandoned and dismantled its internationally respected corporate university in the rush for short term profits.

Innovation & Motivation

Innovation is the heartbeat of invention, of creation, and of moving us to something new and exciting. We love innovation for the same reason we love leaders and entrepreneurs: they take us places we want to go, but didn't know we wanted to go there until we arrived!!

A holistic approach to rewards and motivation has not included the vast research findings in intrinsic motivation. This area of expanded self-determination is a potential treasure trove of options to sustain excited employees at all levels. The sole use of extrinsic rewards for activity versus result demotivates knowledge workers and ignores the intrinsic benefits for the knowledge worker and the organization (Decci, 1995).

Decci points out in, "Why we do what we do" (1995) the issues of control and misunderstanding the cause and effect of traditional reward approach methods over time lead to less motivation not more. The lack of progress and revision to our thinking on how to incorporate intrinsic motivational research continues our industrial age paradigm of employee motivation. I am in full agreement with Decci's statement, "We are asking the wrong questions." An expansion of our thinking and processes to incorporate autonomy and self-determination based on an individual's intrinsic motivation is our next paradigm shift for increased innovation capacity.

We have banded and unbanded compensation levels to streamline the administration and provide flexibility. A good idea at first glance, but often organizations have not provided the necessary job context to assist managers or employees filling in the "to dos" needed to optimize the flexibility of the grade band. Grade banding seems simple, but it requires work in strategies to tactics and goals on the part of a manager to achieve desired performance results. Often this step is not included in the roll out of the job level banding.

The education investments made by the Fortune 100 Corporation in the study developed leaders who respond to knowledge workers with a Dual moral orientation approach. Knowledge workers flourish under Dual moral orientation of their leaders. The characteristics of the Dual modality and knowledge worker motivation were interwoven throughout the research on knowledge workers. Focus on productivity, lifelong learning, and career development motivate this growing group of employees. (Drucker, 1968, 1992; Mohrman & Cummings, 1989; Lawler, 1992;, Von Glinow, 1988). .

Leaders & Corporate Culture

Leaders in today's business environment face many ethical and moral questions. It was so when the study was initially conducted and it is so today. Ethics are key elements in our relationships with colleagues, employees, suppliers, and stakeholders (Wheatley, 1992). Power is generated through these relationships, but what sets their tone, either positive or negative, is the confidence in the leader's fairness and understanding (a combination of Justice-Rights and Care-Connected approaches i.e. the Dual modality).

Hirschman (1970) described two alternatives for members of organizations to resolve their issues. They can either exit the organization when they find they are dissatisfied, or they can voice their concerns in the hope that they will be addressed by their leadership. The exit option is used less when there are fewer jobs available to move to. This results in a third option, dissatisfied employees staying due to lack of economic choices. A knowledge worker without choice feels controlled and unmotivated eliminating the self-determination aspect beneficial to employees and organizations (Deci, 1995).

A culture of obedience rather than innovation emerges in corporations once seen as the seedbeds of ideas, creativity, and breakthrough technology with a reputation for excellence. This is not a surprising outcome because the degree of individual effectiveness is based, in part, on the feelings people have about their organizations (Lawler, 1992; Schein, 1985). Phrases such as, “this is not my job” or “we tried that before” are not the phrases uttered by high performing, innovative, energized knowledge workers.

Company cultures of the industrial age focused on the optimization of the machine with the worker is viewed as an undervalued cost item. The information age parallels this approach when a company’s culture focuses on the optimization of the process diminishing or eliminating investments in knowledge workers. This sub-optimization of knowledge workers concurrently sub-optimizes the innovation potential of the company.

The successful corporations of today embrace Mintzberg’s (2007) definition: “Corporations are social institutions-communities. They function best when committed human beings work in cooperative relationships under conditions of respect and trust.” He goes on to point out, “Destroy this and the whole institution of business collapses.”

Many corporations on a success path in the late 1990's, such as the corporation in this study, mirrors Mintzberg's outcome when the social contract between employees and the corporate leaders is unilaterally altered. The change of leadership at the top, hesitancy to move out on new products, and the breaking of the social contracts with all levels of employees resulted in a free falling culture without a unified direction.

The elimination of the corporation's internal university, which functioned as a culture unifier and innovation incubator for the company, set businesses into individual survival mode. As businesses were sold, further cultural chaos emerged. Today this corporation with a history of inventing new industries is less than one-fourth the size it was during this study.

What's next?

Driving a car by looking in the rearview mirror is a dangerous practice. Looking at where you are going versus where you have been requires the expansiveness of a windshield not the constraints of the small hindsight mirror. Exciting times are ahead for leaders and companies who pioneer new ways to integrate the human capacity of resilience, expanded applications of motivation, and broader models of collaboration.

The explosion of information access through the internet and social media provides an informal look into the thoughts and ideas of today's leaders and professionals. The instantaneous access to media events around the world reinforces the globalness or our interconnectivity as people, cultures, and businesses.

Social Media facilitates the traffic flow of vast information exchange activity is obvious, but the long term impact is less clear. The visibility into personal lives impacts careers as never before. A paradox exists between the missing factual knowledge of many professionals and their willingness to express personal opinion as fact on topics is often reflected in online forums such as LinkedIn and blogs.

Social media empowers individuals to speak up on one hand while concurrently facilitating the stealth reader who is a passive voyeur. Who, how and what is influencing the masses through this electronic fervor is yet to be clarified. As with most internet beginnings, how to cross over to generating revenue through other than advertising options eludes us at present……and maybe, just maybe that's ok.

The explosion of online education through social media, YouTube, blogs, and websites is already having an impact on education at all levels. The for-profit aspect to higher education alive in all university settings will be challenged to redefine the mode and value for the degree seeking knowledge worker beyond the current models.

Our future is full of pioneering possibilities for those willing to step out….. not being constrained by errors of the past or trying to squeeze the last dollar out of a dead idea……but creating visions for knowledge workers to rally and do what they do best……create and innovate!!

References:

Deci, E. L.,(1995). **Why we do, What we do: Understanding self-motivation**. Penguin Books

Drucker, P., (1992). Managing for the future. Truman Tally Books.

Guglielmino, P.J., & Guglielmino, L.M., (1988). Self-directed learning in business and industry: An information age imperative. In Self-directed learning: application and theory. H.B. Long & Associates, eds. University of Georgia, Department of Adult Education.

Hirschman, A.,(1970). Exit, voice, and loyalty. Harvard University Press.

Lawler, E. (1992). The ultimate advantage. Jossey-Bass.

Lin, Justin Yifu, **The China Miracle Demystified**. Paper prepared for the panel on "Perspectives on Chinese Economic Growth" at the Econometric Society World Congress in Shanghai, August 19, 2010

Lim, Linda. Asia 2000. The China Business Review (1997).

Mintzberg, H., How Productivity Killed American Enterprise. Harvard Business Review (July, 2007).

Mohrman, S. A., & Cummings, T.G., (1989). Self-designing organizations: Learning to create high performance. Addison-Wesley.

Prestowitz, C., (2010) **The Betrayal of American Prosperity**. Free Press

Sanders, J., "America must learn from those that Emerged from the Recession's Ashes". Economy in crisis: American's economic report daily (October, 22, 2010)

Schein, E.H., "Reassessing the "Divine Rights" of Managers". Sloan Management Review. 63 (Winter, 1989).

Von Glinow, M., (1988). The new professionals: managing today's high-tech employees. Ballinger Publishing Company.
Wheatley, M.J., (1992). Leadership and the new science. Berrett-Koehler, Publishers, Inc.

Moral Orientation Leadership: a comparative study

Abstract

Moral Orientation of the Senior Leadership in a Fortune 100 Corporation

This study investigated the moral orientation of senior leaders within a Fortune 100 Corporation. Leaders' responses to a moral orientation survey were categorized as Care-Connected, Justice-Rights, or Dual moral orientation. The impact of age, gender, ethnicity, education, years in management, years in the corporation, working experience with multiple employers, and working experience at other business units were analyzed for potential correlation to moral orientation responses. This study was then compared to Carolyn Desjardins' moral orientation study of college presidents.

TABLE OF CONTENTS

LIST OF TABLES

Moral Orientation Leadership: a comparative study

CHAPTER ONE: INTRODUCTION

Today, the world is the market, the consumer is a global citizen, and business alliances are complex. Corporations are being judged by how they respond to the global market, the global environment, and the global worker.

To meet the rapidly changing technology and business environment, tomorrow's organizations will have to be leaner, flatter and move faster to survive. The most successful organization will function as adaptive systems (Rummler & Brache, 1990; Wheatley, 1992; Manz, 1990; Drucker 1992; Galbraith, 1989). An organization will either adapt to the rapidly changing environment or cease to exist. Collaborative leadership is the key variable in effectively predicting and proactively coping with this dynamic business environment.

Statement of the Problem

There are three dynamics currently converging in industry that influence leadership requirements: evolving participative organizational cultures, changing demographics of the workforce from production to knowledge workers, and the changing role of leadership from command and control to facilitators of learning.

Participative Organizational Cultures

Many corporations such as General Motors Corporation, Motorola, Ford Motor Corporation, Cummins Engine Company, Tektronix, Harley Davidson Corporation, General Electric Company, LTV Steel Company, Caterpillar, Inc., IDS, Boeing Company, Polaroid, Inc., and Hewlett Packard, Inc., to name a few, have been experimenting with various forms of collaborative, participative, team-based cultures. The transition from command and control cultures to horizontal participative cultures has been complicated by the lack of awareness and understanding of the differences that exist between persons. An example of this is the balancing of gender related traits that involve a person's moral response to leadership issues.

Research has shown that more men respond from a concept of what is just, right, and remain separate to be objective, while a majority of women respond from a more "care connected" moral orientation with an emphasis on maintaining connection (Gilligan, 1982; Lyons, 1988, Desjardins, 1994). Balancing the Justice-Rights leadership style of hierarchy with the Care-Connected leadership style of inclusion is essential in participative cultures. This lack of awareness has caused misunderstanding that limits attaining the full productivity expected when beginning these cultural transitions.

Changing Workforce Demographics

Future organizations will be diverse, with significantly larger numbers of women, people of color, individuals from different generations, and knowledge workers. It will be increasingly important to understand and honor personal differences in lieu of measuring all individuals against one predetermined set of rules or norms.

The transition from production workers of the Industrial Age to knowledge workers of the Information Age places different expectations in the intrinsic employment contract between the employee and the employer. Knowledge workers are typically well educated, focused on a career versus a specific employer, and motivated by the challenge of the job. Additional expectations include a sense of personal contribution, accomplishment, and the autonomy of the work environment. These work perspective changes challenge the effectiveness of the traditional hierarchy model and emphasize the importance of the moral horizontal inclusive model.

Leaders as Facilitators of Learning

The transition from the Information Age into the Learning Age will require managers and leaders to increase the amount of care-connected mentoring in order to create a learning environment of everyone teaching and everyone learning.

The converging of these dynamics is generating an accelerated need to expand beyond the Justice-Rights moral orientation to include a larger Care-Connected moral orientation approach to leadership. Establishing professional learning communities within agile organizational systems is the competitive advantage for business of the next millennium (Mohrman & Von Glinow, 1988; Shrivastava, 1983; McGregor, 1960; Drucker, 1968, 1992).

The Purpose of the Research

The purpose of this research is to assess the current levels of Justice-Rights and Care-Connected leadership characteristics being utilized within the senior management of a Fortune 100 firm recognized for its progress in total quality management. The need for a balanced approach to leadership decision making through the merging and understanding of moral orientations of the leadership core is essential to the agility of the corporation in responding to the global market, in attracting and retaining highly talented diverse knowledge workers, and in continuing to increase the productivity of the organization.

This research will also compare the leadership moral orientation of a Fortune 100 firm with a study of college presidents to determine if moral orientation differences exist between industry leadership and education leadership.

Research Questions

If one looks at the senior management in a modern, progressive, global, quality-oriented corporation, are there likely to be equal application of leaders in Care-Connected moral orientation and Justice-Rights moral orientation?

The following two hypotheses will be explored in this research to address the main research question: (1) There is a statistically significant difference in the moral orientation of females and males and (2) The percentage of Care-Connected leaders is higher in Desjardins' (1989) study of college presidents than in the senior leaders studied in this dissertation.

Definition of Terms

Moral Orientation. A dualistic approach to thinking about moral problems: The Justice-Rights and Care-Connected approaches are ingrained in the relationships between oneself and others. Justice-Rights relationships are organized in elements of equality, reciprocity, and autonomy. Care Connection relationships are organized in elements of cooperation, empowerment, and nurturance (Gilligan et al, 1988).

Balanced Moral Orientation. Someone seeking or valuing both care and justice; Moral balance concerns spontaneously switched back and for the between the Justice-Rights orientation and the Care-Connected orientation to solve moral concerns in both modes (Gilligan, 1988).

Care-Connected Moral Orientation. Someone seeking or valuing care; this connotes responsiveness or engagement, a resiliency of connection that is symbolized by a network or web. Moral concerns focus on problems of detachment, on disconnection or abandonment or indifference, and the moral ideal is one of attention and response (Gilligan et al, 1988).

Justice-Rights Moral Orientation. Someone seeking or valuing justice; such relationships are organized in terms of equality, symbolized by the balancing of scales. Moral concerns focus on problems stemming from inequality, and the moral ideal is one of reciprocity or equal respect (Gilligan et al, 1988).

Culture. A pattern of basic assumptions—invented, discovered or developed by a given group as it learns to cope with its problems of external adaptation and internal integration—that has worked well enough to be considered valid and, therefore, to be taught to new members as the correct way to perceive, think and feel in relation to those problems (Schein, 1989).

Leadership. The act of establishing the future direction or vision of an organization or group of people; aligning, inspiring, and motivating others to follow and creating the environment to support others in the transition to the desired future (Block, 1987; Kotter, 1990).

Superleadership. A set of behaviors which focus the results of leadership on helping followers to develop the necessary work and self-leadership in order to be able to contribute more fully to the organization (Manz & Sims, 1989).

Self-Leadership. The influence we exert on ourselves to achieve the self-motivation and self-direction we need to perform. The process of self-leadership consists of an array of behavioral and cognitive strategies for enhancing our own personal effectiveness (Manz & Sims, 1990).

CHAPTER TWO:
RESEARCH AND RELATED LITERATURE REVIEW

The purpose of the research and related literature review is to establish the rationale for conducting the research. There are four major literature areas covered in this section: 1. The orientation of moral reasoning, 2. Collaborative organizational cultures, 3. Knowledge workers, and 4. The changing role of leaders. The moral reasoning literature areas relevant to the future leadership needs of an organization are also reviewed.

The Orientation of Moral Reasoning

This review of moral reasoning or orientation will cover the development of moral orientation and the behavioral impact of moral orientation.

Piaget laid the research groundwork for the cognitive-development perspective or moral orientation through the use of semi clinical interviews (Piaget, 1964).

Unlike the psychoanalytic and behaviorist approaches that view morality as conformity to social norms, the cognitive-developmental process emphasizes children's active participation through reasoning about moral issues. Social experiences, physical experiences, and the maturation process shape a child's conceptions of justice and fairness (Piaget, 1965; Kegan, 1982). This process is described by stages loosely based on the chronological age of the child but demonstrated by logic the child uses in solving moral problems.

There are two stages of moral development in Piaget's work: the heteronomous stage in which children view rules as the unalterable dictates of authority figures, and the autonomous stage, in which children view rules as flexible procedures established through cooperative social agreement (Piaget, 1965). Piaget demonstrated that children construct ideas about the world quite differently from parents or teachers. This breakthrough lessened the hold that traditional environmentalist held on child development in the early 1900's. Conceptualizing the acquisition of knowledge and mental growth as a more complex process than researchers had thought (Piaget, 1964).

In his early work, Piaget described social role-taking as the mediator of this cognitive development. As his work progressed, equilibration became the dominant explanatory process. Equilibration is the mode of interaction between a person's maturation, physical experience and social experience (Piaget, 1964).

Kohlberg's Contribution to Moral Orientation

In 1963, Kohlberg published a six-stage sequence expanding Piaget's basic two-stage theory. The six stages are grouped into three levels of moral judgment. At the preconventional level, children judge right and wrong by the consequences of actions. They obey rules to avoid punishment. Morality is governed by the constraint of authority. This is similar to Piaget's heteronomous stage.

In stage two of the first level, reciprocity develops. The child develops a sense of what is fair through equal exchange—"you do this for me and I'll do that for you" (Kohlberg, 1963, 1964). At this basic level, moral orientation is primarily egocentric with the rights of others coexisting with the child's rights (Kohlberg, 1976). Preconventional reasoning declines sharply with age, accounting for 80% of a 10-year-old's moral judgments, 18% of a 16 to 18-yer-old's, and only 3% of a 24-year-old's moral judgments (Kohlberg, 1969; Colby et al, 1983).

At the second level, conventional morality, people focus on interpersonal relationships and social norms. At this stage, individuals follow rules because of the personal consequences associated with rule compliance as part of the existing social system (Kohlberg, 1976). In stage three, a child puts strong emphasis on being a good person in the eyes of self and others, seeking the approval associated with being good. In stage four the right behavior consists of doing one's duty, showing respect for authority, and maintaining the given social order for its own sake (Kohlberg & Gilligan, 1972).

The proportion of conventional moral judgments increases in stages 3 and 4 from 22% at age 10 to almost 90% at age 22 (Kohlberg, 1969; Colby et al., 1983).

At the post-conventional level, moral judgments are based on broad abstract principles. These principles are accepted because they are believed to be inherently right by the individual. In stage five, interpreting and changing the law are seen as options when an ethical reason such as a violation of equality, liberty, or justice exists. The democratic process is emphasized in this stage (Kohlberg & Gilligan, 1972).

In a 20-year longitudinal study of American men (Colby, et al, 1983), they were tested at 4-year intervals between preadolescence and their mid-30s with none of the subjects skipping any stage. Their judgments at any period tended to be remarkably consistent with their peers' level of moral reasoning.

Like Piaget, Kohlberg regarded the clinical interview as the preferred method for studying children's moral development. He also believed that moral development depends on the advances in general cognitive abilities and that moral maturity occurs through invariant sequencing. Each stage evolves from and replaces the preceding one. He introduced the concept of presenting a hypothetical moral dilemma to children and adolescents ad asking them to resolve the dilemma.

The best known of these situations is the Heinz story.

A man whose wife is dying does not have enough money to buy a drug that will save her life. The druggist refuses to lower the price or delay the payment, so Heinz breaks into the drugstore and steals the drug should Heinz have done that? Why or why not? (Kohlberg, 1964)

A person's moral judgment is assessed on the basis of the structure or kind or reasoning used, not the content of the judgment. In other words, a person could receive a high score for saying that Heinz was right or for saying that he was wrong; the score depends on the reasons for the judgment (Kohlberg, 1963, 1964).

Kohlberg studied boys and men as the baseline for descriptions of levels and stages. When girls were tested, they rarely passed the stage of mutual interpersonal expectations, relationships, and conformity under the conventional level (second level, third stage) in their answers. At this stage of moral development a person is aware of others feelings and expectations and places them ahead of self-interests, however, Kohlberg found few people at this level (Kohlberg, 1969).

Gilligan's Contributions to Moral Orientation

Gilligan, an associate of Kohlberg, decided to do a different type of moral study utilizing clinical interviews. However, instead of hypothetical moral dilemmas, she posed the study of judgment and action in real moral dilemmas, she began a study of young men avoiding the draft, but shortly after the study began, the draft was abolished. Arbitron was legalized during this same time frame. Her researched moved to abortion decisions and the inner thinking of the girls in a way that was previously untapped (Gilligan, 1982).

In Gilligan's early work, she described three levels of moral development among women. In the first level, orientation of individual survival, the woman concentrates on what is practical and best for her. Then there is a transition stage from selfishness to responsibility. Here the woman realizes her connection to others, and thinks about what would be the responsible choice in terms of other people as well as herself (Gilligan, 1982).

Level two, goodness as self-sacrifices, is the conventional feminine wisdom. At this level, the woman is sacrificing what she wishes to what other people want, and what they will think of her. She considers herself responsible for her own choices (Papalia & Olds, 1992); Gilligan, 1982). The next transition is from goodness to truth. The woman assesses her decision not on the basis of how others will react to them, but on her intentions and the consequences of her actions. She develops a new judgment that takes into account her own needs, along with those of others. She is seeking both goodness by being responsible to others and honesty by being responsible to self (Gilligan, 1982).

The third level, morality of nonviolence, elevates the injunction against hurting anyone to a principle that givens all moral judgment and action. A woman establishes a moral equity between herself and others. As this point she is then able to assume the responsibly of choice in moral dilemmas based on an objective of hurting no one.

For Care-Connected individuals this stage is critical to their shadow side or fear of abandonment. However, for Justice-Rights individuals, the focus is on the continuation of achieving autonomy or independence (Belenky, 1986; Gilligan, 1982; Desjardins, 1989). In reaction to individuals, primarily women, being considered "stuck" in Kohlberg's conventional level, stage three, Carol Gilligan proposed that women have concerns and perspectives that ware not tapped in Kohlberg's theory and research. Men tend to think more about separation from others to establish independence and autonomy which develops their moral judgment abilities to be just and fair. Women are more concerned with responsibilities which connect them to specific people (Gilligan, 1982).

Moral Orientation Research

Gilligan's work has been echoed in research based on Eriksonian's theory in which women seem to develop identity by not breaking away from others as men do, but through the responsibility and attachment that relationships involve (Chadrow, 1978; Erikson, 1968; Gilligan, 1982). Piagetian and Kohlbergian theories which anchor moral maturity in separation, independence and justice omit the interdependence of adult life and provide a distorted image of the human condition on the whole (Gilligan, et al., 1988). As human beings we want to care and to be cared for (Noddings, 1984). Kohlberg suggested (1969) that one way to potentially increase a woman's stage of moral development would be to engage her professionally outside the home and have her occupy equivalent educational and social positions as men.

To determine the accuracy of this suggestion, Nona Lyons included a sample of professional women in her study of moral orientation and self-definition (1988). The sample consisted of 36 subjects, 18 men and 18 women. Clinical interviews were conducted utilizing structured questions used in the Piaget (1979), Kohlberg (1969), and Gilligan studies (1982). The data were analyzed first by self-definition modes, then for the subjects' moral orientations using real-life moral conflicts, and finally by analyzing the correlation between the two (Lyons, 1988). The findings of this study suggest the potential for professional women working outside the home. Women over the age of 27 show an increase in their justice responses in addressing moral problems, but they continue to favor care response considerations more than rights considerations in resolving conflict (Lyons, 1988).

Three studies conducted by Gilligan and Jane Attanucci (1988) sought evidence that care and justice moral responses would appear by using real-life moral dilemmas versus Kohlberg's use of the hypothetical dilemmas such as the Heinz example. The need for this came from Langdale's findings (1983) that Kohlberg's justice-oriented Heinz dilemma elicits significantly more justice considerations that subject-generated real-life moral dilemmas, or the care-oriented abortion dilemma. Langdale utilized Lyon's coding procedure to code the responses of his sample population. The Gilligan and Attanucci studies consisted of 34 women and 46 men categorized into three age groups, 15 to 22 years, 23 to 34 years, and 35 to 77 years. Two-hour clinical interviews were conducted using Lyon's coding techniques of responses and categorizing the sample based on the frequency of Justice-Rights or Care-Connected responses. In the justice category, 65% of the male responses and 30% of the women's response were reported. In the Care-Connection category, 35% of the female responses and 2% of the male responses were reported. Research subjects responding equally from the Care and Justice moral orientations were 35% of the women and 33% of the men. If women had been excluded from this study, the entire Care-Connected category would have been missed or overlooked (Gilligan & Attanuci, 1988).

The combination of Kohlberg's Justice-Rights research and Gilligan's Care-Connected research depicts two moral perspective which, when linked, provide balance to moral dilemmas by not treating others unfairly and not turning away from the others in need (Gilligan et al., 1988; Kohlberg, 1969).

The conceptualization of care concerns as a moral perspective rather than a deficiency in women's moral reasoning opens the potential for two mature moral orientations. Kohlberg's men exhibited an orientation called Justice-Rights. This orientation explains how the adherence to rules based on varying motivators plays an integral part in establishing moral judgment (Gilligan et al., 1988; Kohlberg, 1984). The Care-Connected orientation motivates moral judgment based on responsiveness, valuing care and fearing abandonment or indifference (Gilligan et al., 1988). These two approaches are not opposites or mirror images. Justice is not uncaring, nor is caring unjust. They simply constitute different ways of organizing the problem that lead to different reasoning strategies, that is, different ways of thinking about what is happening, what to do, and the mode of self-definition (Gilligan et al., 1988). In 1984 Kohlberg described his sixth stage as an integration level of care and justice, but he did not provide details of what care is or how care develops.

The ability to switch orientations and solve problems equally well from the other mode is possible. In about half of the children interviewed, switching either occurred spontaneously or by being triggered by an alternative mode on the part by the interviewer (Gilligan, 1977).

In Desjardins' study of 76 college presidents (1989), 17 % of women and 22% of men were found to have combined modes which show movement between the two moral orientations without prompting. Lyon's study of 36 professionals conducted in 1981 and published in 1988 had differing results in the balanced or combined modes, with no women and one man meeting equal response in each moral orientation.

Moral Orientation, Gender, and Behavior

Two distinct moral judgments exist on different continuums based on relationship approaches. The first is the continuum of inequality---equality. The Justice-Rights orientation values autonomy and reciprocity in interactions or relationships with others. Rules maintain fairness and the basis for reciprocity. Roles are determined by duties of obligation and commitment. Fear of intimacy and oppression are also characteristic of this orientation (Desjardins, 1989; Lyons, 1988).

The second continuum is attachment—detachment. This orientation, Care-Connected, values intimacy and nurturing to alleviate others' burdens or suffering while maintaining a caring and connection in their relationships. Roles are defined through their interconnectedness with others. The fear of isolation and abandonment of self-accompany this orientation. The two in combination shape the experience of self and define the terms of moral conflict (Gilligan, 1982; Desjardins, 1989; Lyons, 1988).

Clearly opposite relationship objectives may lead to different expectations and behaviors toward self and others. Yet they are both different perspectives critical to viewing the world. A more fully developed balance of the Justice-Rights and Care-Connected orientations leads to a more accurate understanding of the interactions between persons and genders (Gilligan, 1982; Desjardins, 1989).

Balanced Moral Orientation

Most people are capable of both modes of moral orientation. Modes are gender-related but not gender-specific (Gilligan, 1982; Gilligan et al., 1988; Lyons, 1983; Desjardins, 1989). More men function primarily in the Justice-Rights mode and more women in the Care-Connected mode, but there are women and men in both modes and a few people who incorporate both modes on a relatively equal basis (Desjardins, 1989; Gilligan, 1982; Smith, 1991). However, a dependency is built into the quest for personal goodness (Kohlberg level2, stage 3). How good one person can be is partly a function of how he/she is received and responded to by another person (Noddings, 1984).

In Gilligan's stages (Gilligan, 1982; Kittay & Meyers, 1987) progress form stage to stage is motivated by the individual's increasing understanding of human relationships and the attempt to maintain one's self without neglecting others.

According to Miller (1976) and Noddings (1984) a woman's sense of self is built around being able to make and maintain connections with others. A loss of relationship is equated to a loss of self. While conflict and guilt are inescapable risks of caring, courage is required to meet these risks. This is consistent with the Belenky et al (1986) study of women moving through stages of developing a sense of individuality and self-esteem establish the connection with others, not at the expense of self, but as a reinforce of self. The overriding fear of abandonment or loss of self through the loss of relationship was found by Desjardins' study (1989) of college presidents. Care-Connected leaders first consider the impact on relationships when making decisions, solving problems, or resolving conflicts within their colleges.

Girls are often observed by teachers to be less outspoken following puberty and less likely to disagree in public. Classroom discussion diminishes and a sense of not wanting to be too smart begins in an attempt to stay connected to their peers (Gilligan, 1984). Sexual activity and teenage pregnancies in part are a result of strategies to care for others or to avoid being alone (Gilligan, 1977).

The Belenky et al. researchers (1986) interviewed women utilizing William Perry's methodology. The phenomenological interviews were open and leisurely, which allowed for the establishment of a rapport between the interviewer and the interviewee. The context was then analyzed repeatedly, paying particular attention to the women's life stories.

Questions were coded for both moral orientation stage and five predetermined epistemological categories. These were:

*1.**Silence**, a position in which women experience themselves as mindless, voiceless subjects to the shims of external authority;*
*2. **Received Knowledge**, a perspective from which women conceive of themselves as capable of receiving, even reproducing, knowledge from the all-knowing external authorities, but not capable of creating knowledge on their own;*
*3. **Subjective Knowledge**, a perspective from which the truth and knowledge are conceived of as personal, private, and subjectively known or intuited;*
*4. **Procedural Knowledge**, a position in which women are invested in learning and applying objective procedures for obtaining and communicating knowledge; and*
*5. **Constructed Knowledge**, a position in which women view all knowledge as contextual, experience themselves as creators of knowledge, and value both subjective and objective strategies for knowing (Belenky, Cinchy, Goldberger, & Tarule, 1986).*

The development of voice for women can be correlated to moral development. Constructed knowers would be at Gilligan's third level of moral development, taking active responsibility for moral choices, while making new connections between knowledge areas. In the moral context she is establishing equality between herself and others, while in the cognitive context, she is experiencing her ideas being validated through the interest of others, and uses herself as an instrument of understanding (Gilligan, 1982; Belenky et al., 1986).

Moral Orientation in Action

A real-life example of the Justice-Rights orientation can be seen in "The Case of the Speluncean Explorers" (Fuller, 1949).

Five members of the Speluncean Society set out to explore a deep cave; a fall of rick completely blocked the only entrance; a large rescue party started to tunnel through the rock, but the work was heavy and dangerous. Ten workmen were killed in the rescue attempt. On the twentieth day of their imprisonment radio contact was established and the trapped men asked how long it would take to free them. Another ten days were estimated as the minimum necessary.

They asked for medical advice on the sufficiency of their rations and learned that they could not hope to survive for ten days more. They then asked if they could hope to survive if they consumed the flesh of one of their party and were told, reluctantly, that they could, but no one—priest or physician or philosopher—was willing to advise them on what to do. On the thirty-second day of their entombment the blocked entrance was pierced and four men walked out.

They said that one of them, Roger Wetmore, had proposed the solution of eating the flesh of one of the party, had suggested the choice be made by throwing dice, and produced a die that he happened to have with him. The others eventually agreed and were about to put the plan into action when he, Roger Wetmore, withdrew, saying that he preferred to wait another week. However, they went ahead, made this throw on his behalf, and he then being indicated as the victim, they killed and ate him. (Douglas 1986)

These men were put to a jury trial and found guilty of murdering Roger Whetmore. During the appeal there were five judges who ruled on the actions of the survivors. The judges perspectives and decision reflect characteristics of Care-Connection and Justice-Rights moral orientation as described by Gilligan (1982, 1987, 1988), Kohlberg *1969), and Desjardins (1989).

The first judge upheld the jury's guilty decision. His perspective is based on his comparison of the facts of the case as weighed against the letter of the law. This is the key component of Justice-Rights moral orientation being demonstrated at a preconventional stage one comparison (Kohlberg, 1963, 1964). He did suggest clemency, which reveals a movement to the conventional morality level stage three, in which shared agreements take precedent over individual interests. The judge's focus on the letter of the law could be seen as a contract view of justice, but the recommendation for clemency potentially moves this judge's decision making to a rational choice position (Rawls, 1971).

The second judge responded form both Justice-Rights and Care-Connected moral orientations. He proposed that they be acquitted for two reasons. First, that the men were trapped, and removed geographically from the force of the law. This attempt to redefine the rules of legal jurisdiction would provide the judge with justification for his position, placing this at a preconventional level. If the judge were to attempt to reach this conclusion motivated from his concern for the defendants, then his could be a Care-Connected transition step between Gilligan's conventional and post-conventional level by merging the consequences of his actions and the responsibility of the decision to others well-being.

Although the outcome of this point alone would take into consideration a portion of the circumstances of the men, it does not abandon the "rules first" thinking which is characteristic of the Justice-Rights moral orientation. Instead, rules are redefined to justify the allowance for an acquittal. This connects the theory of justice with the theory of rational choice (Rawls, 1971) at the transitional level through the classification of the defendants to be outside the society (while underground) and allowing for the development of choosing of alternative of behavior which best suited their situations (Kohlberg, 1963, 1964).

His second reason for acquittal suggested that since 10 workmen's lives had been sacrificed in the rescue, it the defendants were guilty of murder, then the rescue organizations should be prosecuted for ordering the rescue. This was another attempt to change the legal jurisdiction rules instead of changing the moral orientation to one of considering what's best for all. The judge's concern for moral equity between the rescuers and the defendants depicts Gilligan's post conventional level of nonviolent morality. Finally, this judge differentiated between the letter of the law and the interpretation of its purpose, an excellent example of post-conventional moral decision making, as the group followed a universal ethic of survival of many through the sacrifice of this one (Kohlberg, 1964).

The third judge, in solid Justice-Rights mode, agreed with holding the defendants responsible to the letter of the law. This was a classic preconventional level stage one judgment: obedience to the law, or punishment as the consequence.

The fourth judge concluded that the defendants were innocent. He believed that men are ruled by other men, not by words or abstract theories. In this Care-Connected conventional level which outlines goodness as self-sacrifice, he viewed their behaviors as what was best for all concerned (except of course for Roger) and that self-sacrifice is sometimes necessary for the benefit of others (Gilligan, 1982; Gilligan et al., 1988).

The last judge was also in favor of acquittal. He believed that motives and emotions are what matter and that it would be outrageous to convict these men after all the horrors they had endured. In his honoring of emotional truth, this judge demonstrated his Care-Connected made by focusing on the intimacy, climate, and interactions the men were enduring in the cave. Their actions could be seen as preconventional in Gilligan's stage theory. Their focus was on individual survival based on the recommendation of the ultimate victim (Gilligan, 1982).

The Justice-Rights judges in this case analyzed the defendants' moral and personal autonomy based on the social contract established by society. However, the true Justice-Rights tradition, a group of people could consent to redefine the social order based on a change in the social context of their situation (Rawls, 1971; Kittay & Meyers, 1987). This would be validated in the post-conventional level (Kohlberg, 1964).

The Care-Connected judges first analyzed the situation and the defendants' state of emotion being in the context of their decision making. The law was a secondary consideration. Roger's recommendation for one of them to sacrifice himself in order to save the others could be argued as being initiated from the conventional level in Gilligan's (1982) stages.

Organizational Cultures

The business environment in which today's for-profit organizations operate is a continual white water rapids experience. The current environment of change requires organizational leaders to consciously respond to cultural development and management as one of their key responsibilities (Schein, 1985). Organizational cultures are real, visible, and the basis for the performance of both the individuals within the culture and the organization as a whole. The degree of individual effectiveness is based, in part, on the feelings people have about their organizations (Lawler, 1992; Schein, 1985).

Industrial Age: Justice-Rights Cultures

Traditional management acts of controlling, directing, and ultimate decision making with a hierarchical focus are noncompetitive blocking behaviors in collaborative cultures (Galbraith, 1989, 1990; Rummler & Brache, 1990; Manz, 1990). This Justice-Rights management behavior was established during the Industrial Revolution as a necessity in transitioning the rural worker into regimented factory life (Kessler-Harris, 1981). The business culture which emerged as a result of the industrialization movement was Justice-Rights based, focused on insuring strict adherence to the authority of management.

Current High Performance, Collaborative Cultures

Today, many organizations, large and small, are looking into high performance or self-directed work teams to latten their management structures and empower their workforce to achieve competitive advantage (Osburn, 1990). Organizational culture based on these principles moves the policies and values away from the management control norm of the industrial age to a more inclusive set of principles (Lawler, 1992). This transition requires a more interdependent Care-Connected environment be established to accomplish business objectives.

Dynamic networks are established through partnerships, strategic alliances, and cartels. Integration and relationship building and such skills are areas of expertise that are required in order to make these new organizations successful (Snow, Miles, & Coleman, 1992; Karljic, 1983; Kanter, 1994; Galbraith, 1989; Mohrman & Von Glinow, 1988). Care-Connected leaders build inclusive web-like organizations which utilize highly participative decision making processes and focus on establishing relationship oriented cultures (Desjardins, 1989). Open environments with free flowing information assist in facilitating faster adaptability to business or market conditions. An organization's ability to redesign itself is critical in order to achieve a continual adaptation to the global business environment necessary for growth and survival (Weick, 1977; Mohrman & Cummings, 1989; Wheatley, 1992).

Keeping pace with the ongoing need for innovation can only occur if organizational strategic decision making is opened to include input and influence from technical contributors throughout the organization (Grey & Gelfond, 1990; Mohrman & Von Glinow, 1988). Care-Connected leaders, through their inclusionary style, are well suited to lead this type of organization.

Horizontal organizational theories provide linkage in adaptive organizations (Kaplan & Murdock, 1991). Horizontal cultures re-prioritize the processes within an organization. This approach views a company as consisting of 3 or 4 core processes, not functions and hierarchies. The power of this structure is that it captures cross-functional interdependencies and links improvement efforts to a shared set of strategic objectives (Rummler & Brach, 1990; Kaplan & Murdock, 1991; Kanter, 1994; Galbraith, 1989). Cross-functional interdependence grows and prospers through the building of relationships and influence (Care-Connected) versus hierarchical position power that is based on control and chain of command (Justice-Rights) (Hamel & Prahalad, 1990; Block, 1987). In hierarchical organizations, cross-functional groups work for the betterment or survival of one functional silo rather than the business as a whole.

In horizontal organizations customers and employees become a higher priority than internally focused functional alignments and hierarchical empire building. Functions are collaborative interacting subsystems. Their success is linked through functional contribution to the system as a whole. Horizontal organizations believe that employees should be rewarded for their contributions regarding task completion and decision making (Lawler, 1971, 1984; Mohrman, Mohrman, Worley, 1992). These new organizations have much in common with the Care Connected moral orientation.

Changing Workforce Demographics: Knowledge Workers

High technology knowledge workers are expected to make up a larger percentage of the American workforce by the year 2000 than any other time in history. A characteristic of these workers is that they have a far greater interest in their careers than in the organizations that employ them (Von Glinow, 1988). The emerging population of knowledge workers has profound implications on traditional hierarchical systems of organizations. Their expectations require an adjustment to the contract between employees and employers. Their knowledge will be highly sought after as intellectual assets. Focus on productivity, lifelong learning, and career development are keys to motivating this growing group of employees.

Knowledge as Organizational Assets

People's talents are the intellectual assets of an organization, and this talent directly supports the business's core competencies, competition for resources within most organizations is intense. Often the best people are "hidden" away to protect their contribution to their existing assignments. This has the potential to create an overall organizational loss should their talent be require by another business unit (Prahalad & Hamel, 1990).

To insure that employees are perceived as critical corporate assets to the core competencies, management must retain the ability to reassign individuals to protect the overall competencies of the organization. Hierarchies and decentralized organizations tend to reinforce sub optimization and competition, rather than unification and collaboration.

Organization knowledge resides within individual decision-makers, and in the organizational policies and procedures (Shrivastave, 1983). Industrial-age organizations relied exclusively on managers to make the decisions and develop policies and procedures. The manager's role as a key component in these activities was the value they added to the business. Managers were the knowledge workers of this age. In information-age organizations, however, many employees make technical, problem solving decisions. The knowledge worker has a much higher educational and experience level. What was once management's key contribution in decision making based on higher education and experience is now redundant with the contribution of the knowledge workers they are managing (Drucker, 1968, 1992; Mohrman & Cummings, 1989; Lawler, 1990).

Knowledge Worker and Employer Partnership

The American worker typically works a basic schedule of 2080 hours a year. A conservative estimate of 20% overtime adds 400 hours to time spent in the work setting (Bradford & Raines, 1992). Knowledge workers are spending more time in work related activities than any other activity in their lives. These workers are better educated and expect to have more say in decisions that affect their day-to-day work lives and seek greater personal satisfaction in the workplace.

The implicit psychological contracts between employees and employers are established through reactions to work arrangements which are driven by company policies (Lawyler, 1992). A wide range of relationships within the organization set the cultural climate which reinforces implicit behaviors many times unknown or difficult to determine without a mentor's assistance. The individual's capacities for learning, potential for motivation, and loyalty are the employee's side of the implicit contract and are key responsibility areas for employees to bring to the employee-employer partnerships (Passmore, 1988; Von Glinow, 1988; Thoma, 1990).

The visible elements of this contractual relationship include performance measurement practices and career paths. For knowledge workers, career paths are expected to be linked to their output as a demonstration of their capabilities as outline in their job descriptions. Rewards are expected to be both intrinsic and extrinsic, aligning the type of reward to the outcome reached. Selection practices set the initial contract expectations through the data mutually shared by both the employer and the perspective employee during the interview process (Lawler, 1992; Schein, 1985). Development processes, job enlargement, and job enrichment should reinforce the expectations outlined both during the interviewing process and when the performance is being evaluated. In each of these elements, managers have direct roles to play in the organization.

Knowledge workers tend to view the traditional chain of command and authority-based culture in organizations as odd. What matters to them is whether or not the person above them is helpful to their careers. They are willing to fit into a hierarchy only if they perceive they will get something to improve their careers in return (Bradford & Raines, 1992; Von Glinow, 1988; Thomas, 1990). This reciprocity focused moral reasoning on the part of knowledge workers indicates a preconventional, stage two level of development in the Kohlberg model.

In collaborative cultures, knowledge workers should be reasoning at the post-conventional level concurrently I the Kohlberg and Gilligan models. For organizations to be successful, workers must be innovative and spontaneous in order to achieve organizational objectives that go beyond traditional role specifications (Katz, 1964; Mealcher, 1980. This is difficult in hierarchies that operate on a preconventional Justice-Rights moral reasoning level governed by the constraint of authority. To achieve the open-dynamic environments necessary for active innovation, the addition of Care-Connection open communication and interconnectedness among managers, employees, and the organization is essential.

Knowledge Worker Productivity

According to Karune's study (1985) of engineering productivity, there is a range between 30%-70% of an engineer's total decision-making that is autonomous, or up to them without the overview of managerial constraints, be they direct through verbal directions or indirect through policies and procedures. This range of freedom in the workplace is not typically characteristic in hierarchical organizations, which are Justice-Rights based due to their focus on control and rule adherence (Kohlberg, 1969; Fisher, 1993).

When autonomy or total work freedom exceeds 70% the engineers become less productive. This suggests that 100% freedom or the absence of Justice-Rights rules or control is not optimal for engineering productivity. Therefore, a balanced leader approach of setting a number of well chose rules couples with nurturing and mentoring from the Care-Connected leadership approach provides an optimal leadership blend or influencing an engineer's productivity (Torbert, 1991). If the individual has considerable influence in the decision making process, performance was high. Clearly, knowledge workers need to be sold not told (Bradford & Raines, 1992; Von Glinow, 1988; Lawler, 1990). Motivating knowledge workers is a complex balance between Justice-Rights and Care-Connected approaches.

Knowledge Workers as Learners

Success in the marketplace increasingly depends on learning, yet most people don't know how to learn (Argyrus, 1991). Several studies link self-directed learning and performance on the job (Guglielmino and Gugliemino, 1988). This linkage was stronger on rapidly changing jobs or jobs requiring a significant amount or creativity or problem solving.

Knowledge workers are highly educated, autonomy-seeking, and career oriented (Drucker, 1988; Mellander, 1993; Von Glinow, 1988). They engage in knowledge exchange as the currency of trade and pursue intellectual and technical challenges. They join a firm because of the challenge of the work and management's practices.

Many professionals are self-directed learners (Cross, 1981). The self-directed learners are independent, with a high degree of curiosity. They are persistent learners who accept responsibility, and are not stopped by problems. Traditional education settings under value independent individual learning and overvalue learning received from authority figures (Guglielmino and Gugliemino, 1988).

Unlocking the key to every employee's self-development is critical today, as self-developers are defined by values rather than by age. While younger professionals are more prevalent in a general population sample, this is probably not a reflection on the more mature worker, but a result of poor management practices. Industry's fixation on prepackaged classroom training versus self-directed learning process underutilizes human innovation (Knowles, 1975; Guglielmino and Gugliemino, 1988).

Knowledge Worker Motivation

Understanding the motivation of high tech employees is key to insuring the retention of talented employees. A 7 year data collection study of companies with a 50% knowledge worker base was conducted by the Center for Organizational Effectiveness at the University of Southern California. The data collected revealed that the motivation for these workers was not primarily for financial reasons, but for intrinsic rewards such as job content, work environment, stay ahead of the pack, and personal recognition for making a difference (Von Glinow, 1988).

The "me-generation" expects proper recognition in dollars, challenge, advancement, respect and authority (Grey & Gelfond, 1990: Mohrman, Mohrman, & Worley, 1992; Von Glinow, 1988). To motivate self-developers, they must be given opportunities to develop marketable skills, expand their knowledge, or improve their well-being through learning experiences such as travel abroad (Maccoby, 1988).

The new generation of knowledge workers is motivated to succeed in both family life and career. Balance of work and personal life determines how much of themselves to invest in the workplace. They dislike bureaucracies and are not motivated to please the boss so they will be promoted. They do not want to turn the workplace into a supportive family. The primary objective of this mobile group is to look for jobs that develop business and social skills; their career advancement expectations are based on competence and knowledge. They enjoy new people, experiences, and challenges (Maccoby, 1989).

Lateral performance management has a more positive effect than does manager input. It makes the evolution of knowledge worker teams more natural than originally thought. Knowledge worker teams seek accolades. They are attracted to organizations which have high collegial standards, and progressive inclusive management practices (Lawler, 1984; Mohrman, Mohrman, & Worley, 1992; Von Glinow, 1988). These team-based cultures with a more horizontal Care-Connected moral orientation are more likely to appeal to this kind of employee.

Career Development Motivation

Organizations that facilitate career development emphasize such characteristics as achievement, excellence, innovation, risk-taking, and self-development. Career development and choices are an integral part of a knowledge worker's motivation and learning paradigm. Career development leading to career progression can mean the difference between a highly valued technologist staying with a company or moving on (Dalton & Thompson, 1977; Driver, 1979; Grey & Gelfond, 1990). As competition for key technical talent grows, the ability to attract, retain, and develop these individuals is key to both the success of the organization and the satisfaction of its employees.

McKinnon (1987) conducted a study of a large research and development organization. Questionnaires were returned by 367 participants in three divisions. The response rate was 80%. The instrument contained questions on problem solving approaches, leadership characteristics, job characteristics', organizational opportunities, their career preference, and their perceptions about reward practices.

Based on the answer to the career question, the sample was then classified into managerial ladder, technical ladder, and project oriented (migration from project to project) categories. Two-thirds said their career progression has been from one interesting project to another (McKinnon, 1987).

The demographic profile of "Project people" was different from the other two groups. They were older, with more experience in the company and in their field. They seemed to stay more current on professional developments through technical journals. All groups valued autonomy, freedom, the chance to work with bright colleagues, and the opportunity to work on challenging projects.

Respondents in the technical ladder group valued working on professional problems, while respondents in the managerial group valued opportunities that could lead to organizational advancement. Professionals with different perceptions of their careers had very different expectations of an organization. This directly impacts the most appropriate leader's moral orientation for the employee. An engineer pursuing the technical ladder will spend the majority of his/her time resolving technical issues that are driven by rules and hierarchal thinking. A Justice-Rights leader who is goal oriented and focused on analysis and definition could be appropriate for such a technologist (Desjardins, 1989; Karunes, 1985; Dalton & Thompson, 1977). Knowing what ladder the engineer is pursuing is helpful in understanding the sources of his/her motivation (Dalton et al., 1977; Driver 1979).

Changing Role of Leadership

Leaders in today's business environment face many ethical and moral questions. Ethics are key elements in our relationships with colleagues, employees, suppliers, and stakeholders (Wheatley, 1992). Power is generated through these relationships, but what sets their tone, either positive or negative, is the confidence in the leader's fairness and understanding (a combination of Justice-Rights and Care-Connected approaches).

Consequences of Leadership Status Quo

Justice-Rights and Care-Connection constitute different ways of organizing problems that lead to different reasoning strategies; different ways of thinking about what is happening and what to do (Gilligan, 1987). The expansion of ideas, reasoning, and strategies are key to gaining more from relationships within an organization. Limiting leadership perspectives or style to only one or the other moral orientation inhibits a complete picture being considered with significant organizational consequences.

Hirschman (1970) described two alternatives for members of organizations to resolve their issues. They can either exit the organization when they find they are dissatisfied, or they can voice their concerns in the hope that they will be addressed leadership.

Another organizational consequence is the loss of key information. The focus of information in the Justice-Rights style is in the accuracy of the information and how best to analyze it. The Care-Connected focus adds a dimension of process to insure that the data collection method did not result in loss of information (Wheatley, 1992; Helgesen, 1990).

If leadership only views the right or ethical behavior from a rational-cognitive approach, it fails to share with the employees' mutual feelings, conflicts, hopes, and ideas that influence their eventual choices. The rational approach contains the inherent risk of only sharing the justification for its acts and not what motivates and touches it (Noddings, 1984). This could accelerate the member exit or silence their voice based on the perception that they are not being heard (Hirschman, 1970). The one cared for (in this example the employee) sees the concern, delight, or interest in the eyes of the one-caring (in this example the leadership), feeling the warmth of both verbal and body language. To the cared-for, no act on their behalf is quite as important or influential as the attitude of the one caring (Noddings, 1984).

When the attitude of the one-caring reflects caring, the cared-for glow, grow stronger, and feel not so much that they have been given something, but that something has been added to their lives. This is part of the effectiveness mentoring has with knowledge workers (Noddings, 1984).

The Emerging Voice

Voice is influenced by loyalty. Loyalty is established in knowledge workers by their relationship with their leaders and if the work they are assigned is challenging (Von Glinow, 1988; Bradford & Raines, 1992; Driver, 1979). Care-Connected leaders first consider the voice element. Justice-Rights leaders first consider the fairness of the voice. This is a key difference in listening to the voices in organizations, the timeliness of responding and reacting to their needs could be the difference between exit and developing loyalty (Noddings, 1984; Hirschman, 1970; Morhman & Von Glinow, 1988; Nomikos, 1989).

Leaders tend to exhibit a dominant moral orientation approach, but many do have access to both perspectives (Gilligan, 1977). A person's initial or spontaneous approach to a problem is not necessarily the one which she or he would deem preferable after further consideration (Gilligan et al., 1988). However, people do have a preferred way of seeing, listening, and speaking so that one voice is more readily head or understood by them (Gilligan et al., 1988).

Women as Leaders

The entrance of women into organizations raises the possibility of a different mode of operating as leaders. Kohlberg suggested (1969) that one way to potentially increase women's stage of moral development would be to engage professionally outside the home and occupy equivalent educational and social positions as men. To determine the accuracy of this suggestion, Nona Lyons included a sample of professional women in her stud or moral orientation and self-definition (1988). The sample consisted of 36 subjects, 18 men and 18 women. Clinical interviews were conducted utilizing structured questions as used in the Piaget (1979), Kohlberg (1969), and Gilligan studies (1982). The data were analyzed first b self-definition modes, then for the subjects' moral orientations using real-life moral conflicts, and finally by analyzing the correlation between the two (Lyons, 198).

The findings of this study suggest the potential for professional women working outside the home, over the age of 27 shows an increase in their justice responses in addressing moral problems, but they continue to favor care response considerations more than rights considerations in resolving conflict (Lone, 1988).

Sally Helgesen conducted a study of women leaders in 1990 based on a combination of observations and interviews similar to Mintzberg's management research (1973). Her findings show women tend to schedule time for sharing information and structure their companies as networks or grids instead of hierarchies (Helgesen, 1990; Rosener, 1990). They refer to themselves as being in the middle of things rather than being on top. Decisions are typically not made in haste, but after seeking a lot of information from a wide range of individuals. Information flow is encouraged and leaders act as facilitator extracting and directing the pat of data (Helgesen, 1990). As the Belenkey et al. research focused on women finding a voice, women in leadership rely on voice over vision. The voice is essential in communication, but listening is the key to dialogue and interaction (Belenkey et al., 1986; Helgesen, 1990).

Relational Leadership

Another element in today's global organization is the focus place on the leadership alliances, partnerships, and other business relationships. Negotiations in the development and sometime ongoing interactions within business relations are inevitable. The high value women place on interdependence and Care-Connectedness crepe a negotiation climate and strategy that preserves the relationship. The male Justice-Rights approach focused on independence, autonomy, and competition often times creates a climate of negotiation based on winning or beating the opponents, rather than collaborating and building a relationship (Helgesen, 1990; Rosner, 1990; Gilligan, 1987).

Those leadership skills that are valued today have a much larger relationship slant than those required of leaders in the past. Contemporary leaders are encouraged to motivate followers through empowerment, and include stakeholders in decision making creating a circular set of circumstances. These are Care-Connected characteristics and generally practice by women leaders (Desjardins, 1989; Helgesen, 1990). Leadership is dependent on the context of the relationship with the followers, and that context is established by the relationships leaders value (Wheatley, 1992).

In a hierarchically organized setting, employees are communicated to on a need-to-know basis. This puts managers in a tenuous position. First, the manger must become the employee's protector and decide what is important for the employee to know without accessing the employee. Hierarchical communication strategies lead employees to conclude that managers are not telling them the whole story and, eventually, to distrust their motives (Nomikos, 1989; Schein, 1989; Strata, 1989). A protector manager is using Justice-Rights practice of predetermine what to communicate, closely guarding information as a measure of power over the subordinate (Lyons, 1990; Desjardins, 1989).

Building trust is a process based on reciprocity. An employee seeking the trust of a manager needs to exhibit personal responsibility and competence. Managers have to build trust through consistent honest feedback, clarity of communication, and by following through with commitments to employees (Lawler, 1971, 1990; Mohuman & Von Glinow, 1988; Morhman, Mohrman, & Worley, 1992; Osburn, 1990). As trust develops, the role of the manager can evolve from one of primarily providing content expertise, to being the supplier of guidance, mentorship, and mission, vision information (Osburn, 1990; Lawler, 1992; Fisher, 1993).

Decision Making Processes.

Optimal decision making in hierarchies are based on a manager's effort to reduce uncertainty and to increase closure (Bass, 1983). Ideally, organizations expect managers to search for decision alternatives in anticipatory fashion through heuristic or means-ends analysis. In order for managers to conduct such analysis, they must utilize their past experiences, current knowledge, and possess their own problem-solving skills.

For employees to assume decision making responsibilities, current decision makers need to mentor employees to build their skills in information gathering, problem-solving, contextual knowledge, and through lessons learned by the manager through past experience. This employee development should occur prior to transitioning the decision making and throughout the first few new decision cycles. This will instill confidence and trust in the employees' decision making capabilities for both the manager and the employee. Management guidance through the first few decisions builds confidence in employees (Katzenback & Smith, 1993; Lawler, 1992; Fisher, 1993).

Managers' decision making process can be categorized in four approaches: Autocratic decisions are solely leader dependent with no input from subordinates; Consultative decisions open the process of seeking data from subordinates, but the ultimate decision is up to the leader. Joint decisions could be considered group decisions, as the leader brings the issue to the group and through dialogue a joint decision is made; delegation moves the authority and responsibility for decision making to the subordinate without the approval of the leader (Heller & Yukl, 1969); Nannebaum & Schmidt, 1958; Vroom & Yetton, 1973).

These categories show that both types of moral orientation are being actively engaged. For example, the autocratic style of m engagement would tend to be based solely on Justice-Rights orientation at a preconventional or conventional level (Kohlberg, 1969). The consultative and joint decisions would involve inclusion, which are practices of a Care-Connected leader (Desjardins, 1989). The delegation category could utilize moral orientation depending on the leader's direction in framing the decision making expectations and the response made to the decision by the employee.

Managers should follow the same guidelines for delegating decision making as followed in delegating other responsibilities. This includes: 1) determining how much authority is necessary, 2) insuring subordinate comprehension, 3) obtaining subordinate acceptance of responsibilities, 4) motoring subordinate progress, 5) providing assistance and psychological support, and 6) discouraging excessive dependence (Yukl, 1981; Lawler, 1990, 1992; Manz, 1989; Fisher, 1993).

As managers introduce decision making to the team, planning, facilitating, and group process become the manager's focus. Communication during the initial phases of this transition can make or break the successful transition of decision making. Managers will need to provide more strategies for leading others to lead themselves. Manz and Sims (1989) referred to this process as "superleadesrship". This approach moves managers to a supportive role in relationship to employee development versus a directive role in the traditional command and control leadership approaches prevalent in the industrial age. This is a difficult shift for traditional managers and is often perceived as a loss of power and control by them.

The Work of Leaders

Traditional managers spare little time for activities not directly related to their work. To protect them from daily interruptions, they utilize their secretaries as shields. They have difficulty sharing information, and have highly compartmentalized identities separating their roles as manager, father, husband, etc., (Mintzberg, 1989; Helgesen, 1990). The behaviors and work habits that lead to success in the industrial age are significant obstacles in the information age.

Management relates to objects, while leadership relates to people. The information age is leader, not manager driven. Management tasks are important, but must be undertaken in tandem with leadership (Kotter, 1990). Many team-based organizations are moving day-to-day management tasks from managers to self-directed work teams, freeing leaders for strategy development and long-term planning (Fisher, 1992; Godman, Sproull, & Associates, 1990).

Leaders in organizations' making the transition to team based management are concerned about their own job security, and fear losing control of their employees. Employees are hesitant to assume new decision making responsibilities for three reasons: (1) they are not prepared with the proper skills, knowledge or tools to make quality decisions, (2) increased responsibilities accompanied by increased stress piggy backs onto increased decision making, and (3) they do not trust that they will actually be given the authority to execute the decisions they make.

The role of the manager in such organizations involves much coaching, assisting employees in gaining both the skills and confidence to take on new decision making responsibilities (this includes allowing room for failure during the learning period), and nurturing a work environment that supports initiative and individual responsibility (Lawler, 1990, 1992; Manx & Sims, 1990; Osburn, 1990).

To reinforce the move toward participative Care-Connected behavior, management reward systems should focus on mentorship, team, and individual skill development, and personal commitment to continual improvement and renewal (Lawler, 1990; Rummler & Brache, 1990).

An engineering manager, for example, may have a career spread over all four stages. As a manager, she may have the responsibility to develop other engineers who work for her. As an engineer managing a new technical program, she may find herself an apprentice in the new technology, but a colleague while conferring with other mangers on a business unit issues. If she has political influence, she may be sponsoring engineers for promotions or challenging assignments.

Her time may be spread over the four stages, although most of her time is spent in the mentor or sponsor stage. In a team-based culture, her time will be utilized on a leadership team as a colleague with other leaders within the organizations (Osburn, 1990).

Summary

This is the first time these four literature subjects have been brought together. The moral orientation literature acts as an equilibrium that determines the mode of interaction among the other three literature areas: collaborative organizational cultures, knowledge workers, and the changing role of leadership. These areas combine to affect the cognitive capabilities of organizations of the future through their maturation of honoring personal differences and seeking balance between Care-Connected leadership and Justice-Rights leadership.

Many corporations are currently making the transition to team-based collaborative cultures. The intent of these transitions is to add agility and feaster response cycles to the global business environment (Galibraith, 1989; Rummler & Brache, 1990; Osburn, 1990). Knowledge workers are the primary worker of the information age. They are motivated by relationships, challenging work assignments, personal accomplishment, and autonomy (Von Glinow, 1988).

Traditional management approaches prevalent in the industrial age are counterproductive to the information age employees (Drucker, 1992; Lawler, 1990). The leaders of today must be more aware of relationships than ever before. They must bold trust, mentor others, and create work environments that support creativity and initiative (Manz & Sims, 1990; Lawler, 1990, 1992).

Moral development of leaders regarding Justice-Rights and Care-Connected reasoning is critical for long term business success. These moral orientations are gender related not gender specific. Justice-Rights focus on the continuum of equality-inequality. Autonomy and reciprocity in interactions with others are key values for the Justice-Rights leader. The Care-Connected leader is operating along the attachment-detachment continuum. Intimacy and nurturing interactions with others are the key values of a Care-Connected leader. Both approaches are important in creating balanced leadership within organizations.

CHAPTER THREE: METHOD

Organizations are experiencing a workforce in transition, with an increased number of knowledge workers, women, and people of color. Many corporations have initiated some form of participative management practices such as quality circles, self-directed work teams, or a task force. The changes in the work environment resulting from increased employee participation have altered what employees expect from their leaders.

The Justice-Rights command and control style leadership is being redefined to include a Care-Connected focus on employee mentoring, and distributed or decentralized decision making. Leadership style reflects the moral orientation of the leader (Desjardins, 1989; Smith, 1992). The purpose of this study is to determine the current moral orientation of the senior leadership within a business unit of a Fortune 100 for-profit corporation.

Selection Rationale: Fortune 100 Corporation

This for-profit Fortune 100 Corporation has been on a journey of continual improvement in productivity for the past 15 years. Productivity initiatives have focused on the balance between quantitative - qualitative improvement programs.

This balanced approach is reflected in the employee Total Customer Satisfaction card which is carried by all employees. This 2 X 3 inch card lists the corporation's **key beliefs, key goals, and key initiatives**. Its guiding principles are: 1) constant respect for people, and 2) uncompromising integrity in all that we do. All of the key goals and key initiatives have these two key beliefs as the foundations for achievement, and are listed at the top of the card.

Key goals are listed next on the employee card. These outline what the corporation must accomplish **Increased market global market share** reflects the international focal of both today's communications market and the corporation's business objectives. The next item listed is to be the **Best in Class** corporation in all areas. This includes best in class **people, marketing, technology, products, manufacturing, and services**. Here again, this Fortune 100 corporation stresses the interdependencies between people and all the process or functions the corporation offers to customers. The third goal listed is **super financial results**.

Many corporations would list this as their number one goal, but his operation lists this as the third goal. Organizational expectations are to meet the first two goals of increasing global market share and the striving to have best in class people, resulting in superior financial gains. The evolution of such initiative programs encompasses a blend of cycle time, quality, and employee empowerment.

Cycle time programs include 10-fold improvement, 100-fold improvement, and total cycle time. Ten-fold improvements were the first cycle time improvement imitative. Work processes were mapped using basic process mapping techniques. Each step in the map is timed to determine how long it takes to complete eat stage. The steps are then added together to establish a baseline cycle time for the progress. Once the time per process are mapped based on the current work, each process is expected to be reworked to shorten the cycle time by a factor of ten. For example, if the cycle time of a process is 100 hours, then the ten-fold improvement initiative, the cycle time is expected to be shortened to 10 hours. This same process was utilized during the one-hundred fold improvement initiative. Each of these three initiatives focus at doing work faster occurred sequentially.

Although the method for conducting each cycle time initiative was the same, each program reflects the resetting of the goal to complete the work at an even faster more efficient rate. The quality movement within this corporation is measured in sigma (standard deviation from normalized curves). Six sigma refers to having 3.4 errors or defects for each 100 million opportunities for error. This requires 99.99966 percent of the output from any given process must be defect-free, for example, the sigma calculation based on the number of correctly spelled words on a page. One sigma would allow for 170 misspelled words per page. Four sigma would allow for one misspelled word per 30 pages (about one chapter in a book). Six sigma would allow for one misspelled word I all of the books contained in a small library. All major processes are measured against this metric to generate a sigma level.

Product and manufacturing leadership approaches are standardized manufacturing processes and standardized engineering design methodologies.

Participative management within and cooperation between organizations began with the participative management programs. There were two phases on this initiative, one of the earliest corporate wide programs in industry to integrate goal achievement, employee participation in management decision making, and compensation for individuals based on the tam or departments successful in achieving the goals. Currently, various forms of self-directed wok teams are being implemented in business groups and sectors. Team based culture implementation has been a major driver in reformatting old metal models of management practices. Since many employees are knowledge workers, the management process transformation has encompassed both justice-rights and care-connected aspects.

Through the development of empowered cooperation, teams have successfully established relationships which nurture the development of each individual while applying fair and just rules. The balance of power is migratory and fluid, but structured to ensure an organized hand-off. This may appear to be a paradox, fluid yet structured, but the success of teams is increased through this preparation process. Decisions are only shifted from mangers to teams when the teams are prepared to assume both the accountability and responsibility for their outcomes of their decisions. The decision-making hand-off process engages both Justice-Rights and Care-Connected moral orientations concurrently by being concerned for their success while being analytical in assessing their readiness.

Although profit improvement is listed under the key initiatives section of the card, most leaders and employees believe that profit improvements is the outcome of the other four initiatives. Five years ago (1991) all of these programs were under the primary goal of Total Customer Satisfaction.

Senior management champions are identified as each program is implemented. Massive training and awareness, status, and results reporting, and even a pocket card carried by each employee (typically attached to employee badges) has been in use. Each year every employee is expected to attend a minimum of 40 hours of training. This focus on education enables employees to gain personal and professional skills which will aid them in pursuing their career and family interests.

Care-connection extends beyond the typical employee programs found in other corporations, such as medical benefits or pay increases. Employees' families offered opportunities such as science summer camps for elementary children, child care (both well child and sick child), and diverse coursework in parenting, marital relationships, and financial planning. The corporation's community roles include a number of programs such as adopting "at risk" elementary schools. Employees are encouraged to volunteer at these schools in such programs as Junior Achievement, mentoring, guest speaking, and student tutoring. Employee time required for these activities is paid for by the business units when the events coincide with regular work hours.

This balanced focus between and care and respect of employees and the justice sought through uncompromising integrity drive the key goals and key initiatives forward. The results of this balanced approach have led to this for-profit company being among the first recipients of the Malcomb Baldridge Quality Award. It has been identified by **Fortune** magazine as one of the ten best managed corporations, and selected by **Working Woman** magazine as one of the top 100 employers for women in the nation.

By creating a Cared-Connected environment open to diversity, this company has successfully attracted and retained larger numbers of women and minorities than other comparative corporations. There are more female and minority vice presidents at this for-profit Fortune 100 Corporation of similar size.

The company's relationship with employees, their families, and communities is balanced through the initiatives programs which continually drive competition to dramatically improve the current level of performance and productivity necessary to achieve the increased global market share and superior financial growth.

The characteristics of this for-profit Fortune 100 Corporation make it one of the best environments in which to study the moral orientation of leadership as being Justice-Rights, Care-Connected, or Dual, moving with equal ease between Justice-Rights and Care-Connection.

Participants

The pool to be surveyed is made up of senior leaders of a billion dollar business nit within this Fortune 100 Corporation. This business unit consists of three divisions: two commercial divisions, one defense division, and five major staff functional areas: Supply Management, Engineering Support, Computer Integrated Systems Design, Finance, and Human Resources.

The sample consisted of the top four tiers of Manager, E13, E14, E15, and vice presidents. "E" grades range from an E04 entry level professional, to an E26, a senior executive vice president within the business unit used in this research. Participants are either direct chain-of-command leaders or technology leaders. The common descriptors consist of: (1) level within the organization, (2) the same beans group, and (3) the same corporation. In addition, there is a description of gender, age, work location, type of business, length of service with the company, and length of time as a leader.

Procedure

Moral Orientation Research

The conventional approach to moral orientation research is through a five-part, open-ended interview which is conducted in a clinical manner derived from Piaget (1929, 1979). The interview proceeds from structured questions to a more unstructured exploration and clarification of each person's responses. Interview questions were developed to highlight the individual constructs of the experience of self and the domain of morality (Lyons, 1981; Gilligan, 1982; Desjardins, 1989).

The interview data were first analyzed for modes of self-definition, then for the subjects' orientations within considerations of real-life (Lyons, 1981) or leadership (Desjardins, 1989) moral conflicts. The final step is to analyze the data for any existing correlations between the two moral orientations (Justice-Rights and Care-Connection) and presence of third moral orientation, Duality. Dual moral orientation is defined as the moving with equal ease between the Justice-Rights and Care-Connection.

The Moral Orientation Survey (MOS)

The instrument used in this study is a Moral Orientation Survey (MOS). The MOS was developed to assess the dominant moral orientation of each participant. The survey questions resulted from the research on the leadership competency in community college presidents (Desjardins, 1989) as well as the extensive general research in moral orientation (Lyons, 1981; Gilligan, 1982; Belenky et al., 1986).

The MOS consists of two parts. The first part has 27 items composed of two statements—one representing the Justice-Right approach toward leadership and a second representing the Care-Connected approach toward leadership. Participants are asked to circle the one item in each area which accurately describes them and to circle only one of the statements within each question which best describes their leadership approach. Should both statements accurately describes them, they are instructed to select the statement which best describes what they would do first.

To validate the survey used in this research, 10 previous participants of Desjardins' study of college presidents completed the MOS survey based on their moral orientations, as determined by clinical interviews. There were 5 Justice-Rights leaders and 5 Care-Connected leaders in this validation sample. Each question was reviewed to insure that the responses directly correlated with the moral orientations determined in Desjardins' interviews. Questions which did not directly correlate were eliminated.

Desjardins' original study consisted of 76 college presidents. Each participant was clinically interviewed using the Gilligan interview technique formal orientation. There were 38 men and 38 women in her sample. The study consisted of two interrelated sections. The first section categorized the college presidents as being Justice-Rights, Care-Connected, or Dual (an equal blend or Justice-Rights and Care-Connected moral orientation). Fifty percent of the male sample and 17% of the female sample were Justice-Rights in their moral orientation. Care-Connection was found in 28% of the male population and 66% of the female population. The Dual moral orientation style accounted for 17% of the women and 22% of the male population.

Gilligan's results in studying adolescents had different findings that Desjardins' study. Gilligan used a two-category, Justice-Rights moral orientation and Care-Connected moral orientation to segment her findings. Justice-Rights moral orientation accounted for 40% of the females and 60%of the males. The inverse occurred in the Care-Connected moral orientation, with males representing 30% and females representing 70% of the total study group.

The second section of the MOS survey consists of participants' personal histories. There are eight separate questions which provide personal profile data: age, gender, college depress completed, ethnicity, number of years in management, number of years at this corporation, number of different business suits within this corporation worked for, and number of other employers in same career to date. A ninth question regarding the length of time to complete this survey was included for the pilot to determine the how long it takes to complete the MOS. The targeted completion time was less than 30 minutes as reported by the pilot sample participants.

The Research Process

A self-administered anonymous questionnaire was distributed to senior managers of the study corporation. The questionnaire was easy to complete and did not exceed the practical guideline of 20-minute response item. A cover letter and participant consent form accompanied the survey (Appendix A).

The responses were separated into three categories: 1) Justice-Rights orientation, 2) Care-Centered orientation, and 3) Dual orientation. Comparisons of the three groups were then cross-referenced to the supplemental data section of the survey, which as mentioned previously, consisted of eight personal descriptors. The supplemental data are analyzed to determine to what extend correlations exit between moral orientations and these personal factors. For example, was there a correlation between the amount of Care-Connection and the number of years in management?

The data are then analyzed comparing the response trend of participants' response in all three moral orientations. This provides insight into the effects of different management styles, by identifying under what circumstances Justice-Rights leaders respond in a Care-Connected way and vice versa. This is particularly important in the Dual respondents' management style which represents participants who equally apply Justice-Rights and Care-Connected decision making approaches. By understanding the specific of the response by each category, leaders are able to have a more thorough understanding of their primary leadership style in making decision, which can then guide their future leadership development.

The final analysis compares the Moral Orientation Survey results of this research with the traditional clonal interview approach utilized in Desjardins' study of college presidents.

The Research Question

This study has been designed to respond to the following two research questions regarding the blend of Justice-Rights and Care-Connected leadership approaches currently being utilized by senior managers of a Fortune 100 Corporation. First, what is the moral orientation of the senior management in a Fortune 100 Corporation: Second, how does the industry data on moral orientation compare to the leadership orientation of college presidents in the Desjardins' study?

Hypotheses Statements

Hypotheses are centered around the eight supplemental variables listed on page 4 of the Moral Orientation Survey.

H1, Care-Connected moral orientation progressively increases as the age of the leader increases. This hypothesis is influenced by Valliant's research (1977) on the increased need for older men to be more relationship focused than they were when they were younger.

H2, leaders with more education are less Cared-Connected than leaders with less education. In Gilligan's research (1892), she differentiated between Justice-Rights responses and Care-Connected responses of the research participants. If Kohlberg's (1964) stage model is used as the moral orientation norm, the Care-Connected model proposed through Gilligan's research would link at the middle stage. The potential result was described in this hypothesis would be that the higher the leader's education level , the higher the leader's moral orientating as Justice-Rights based according to Kohlberg's stage theory.

H3, Anglo-Saxon leaders are less Care-Connected than non-Anglo-Saxon. My personal experience in consulting with managers is the basis for this hypothesis. There is no direct research at this time in the literature to serve as a comparative for H3.

H4, male leaders are less Care-Connected than female leaders. This hypothesis is based on the research covered in Gilligan's original research (1982), Desjardins' research of college presidents (1989), Nona Lyon's research of professionals (1990) and the Belenky et al research describing women's development (1986).

H5, leaders with multiple employer work experiences are more Care-Connected than leaders with single-employer experiences. The process of being accepted and included as a valid leader in a new organization is the basis for this hypothesis. There is currently no direct research on which to base this hypothesis.

H6, leaders with work experience in multiple basins units are more Care-Connected that leaders with single business unit work experience. Given the overall organizational culture as described in the Selection Rationale scion of this chapter, the culture seems to attempt to balance Justice-Rights and Care-Connected expectations for employees.

H7, leaders with more years working at this Fortune 100 Corporation are more Care-Connected. As in H6, this hypothesis is related directly to the cultural profile of this Fortune 100 Corporation.

H8, leaders with more years in management are more Care-Connected in their moral orientation. This hypothesis is based on my consulting experience. The more experienced leaders have appeared to be more concerned about the inclusion of their employees in decision making.

Limitations of the Study

The limitations of this study occur in four primary areas. First, the potential for a disconnection between the intellectual responses of the participants who are leaders and their actions is not addressed. Each of the participants has been through extensive training and education in the Fortune 100 corporations' initiative programs described in the rational selection section of this paper.

Some of the questions may elicit what may be perceived as subconsciously politically correct responses rather than true responses. The cultural influence of this corporation is typically started with senior leaders championing new initiatives. The thrust for the past ten years has been various forms of participative management of inclusionary management which lends more towards a Care-Connected approach versus a Justice-Rights approach. Senior leaders are trained first in new initiatives and are expected to be the initiative role models. Although this was not anticipated at the beginning of the study, as data was collected, the large number of Care-Connected responses triggered the potential for multiple motivators such as intellectual conditioning through training or politically correct responses based on the evolution of the leaders' role min the transitioning organizational culture.

Secondly, the simple population is only form one business unit within one Fortune 100 Corporation. The responses would not necessarily reflect the corporation's leadership moral orientation in total, limiting its applicability to this particular business unit. The homogeneity of this population could serve as the best indicator of moral orientation within the corporation, based on the length of service of the leaders and the limited experiences they have had as employees or leaders with other corporations and other business units within this Fortune 100 Corporations.

Thirdly, the number of women and minorities in the total leadership population of this business unit does not equal the number of white male leaders. The focus of this research is not limited to gender and minority variables, but to leadership moral orientation of the entire group. To increase the sample of women and minority leaders, more "E" grades would need to be included in the survey participant pool.

Finally, the use of a survey versus a traditional clinical interview regarding moral orientation limits the ability of the researcher to ask more in-depth questions.

CHAPTER FOUR: RESULTS

This study was designed to investigate two research questions regarding the moral orientation of senior leaders in organizations. An understanding of the moral orientation of senior leaders, directors, and vice-presidents of a business unit within a Fortune 100 Corporation was the object of the first set of research questions.

To address the first question, the leaders' responses were categorized as "Care-Connected, Justice-Rights, or Dual moral orientation. The impact of age, gender, ethnicity, education, years in management, years in the corporation, working experience with multiple employers, and working experience at other business units were explored. There are eight supplemental variables found in the Moral Orientation Survey are the basis for eight research hypotheses which introduce each section.

To address the second research question, the results of this study were compared to the college presidents' moral orientation data in the Desjardin's study (1989).

The first section of this chapter is a descriptive profile of the sample responding to the Moral Orientation Survey (MOS) used in this study. The second section contains two methods of quantitative analyses of the data for each of the eight hypotheses. Section one presents an analysis of the survey responses by question to determine any trends in participant responses base on moral orientation modes.

Secondly, comparisons between moral orientation modes and the eight supplemental variables are made to determine the consistency or the trend of responses. The chi-square is used to test the association between the supplemental variables and the moral orientation modalities (Justice-Tights, Care-Connected, Dual to determine which of them are significant. Third, Correlation and Analysis of Variance statistics are calculate to test the relationship between an actual total score on the survey and the supplemental variables.

The last section this chapter compares the senior leadership research of this study and the Desjardins' study of college presidents.

Descriptive Profile

The sample population for this research was composed of 212 leaders from the top three levels of management within a single business unit of a Fortune 100 corporation. One hundred and thirty-eight or 65% of the survey population responded to the Moral Orientation Survey. The majority of the respondents, 88% are Anglo males, approximately 93% are males and 98% are college graduates. The majority of the leaders, approximately 55%, have post-graduate degrees, with doctorates representing 9% of the post-graduate degrees.

The overall work experience of this leadership population has been at this corporation. Approximately 43% have worked only at this corporation; with 17% of the respondents have worked at four or more employers in their careers to date. As the level of the leadership sample increased the number of employers decreased. Sixty percent of the respondents have spent their careers with this Fortune 100 Corporation at the business unit surveyed. Over 50% of the remaining respondents have worked at four or more business units. This is most prevalent in the E13 leadership category. The majority of the total group of leaders, 81% have spent over 10 years of their careers this corporation. Seventy percent of the respondents have over 10 years in management.

Overall, the senior leadership group was most often approximately 49% categorized as Dual moral orientation. Care-Connected moral orientation responses were prevalent in 42% of the leader's responses. The fewest responses (9%) were in the Justice-Rights moral orientation category.

Survey Question Analysis

Reviewing the participants' responses to specific questions, a few interesting results emerged. For example, in question 1, all the Justice-Rights leaders responded with the Justice-Rights response, ("I focus on the outcomes of decision making rather than the process"), but in question 12, all the Justice-Rights leaders circle the Care-Connection option, ("I work to identify issues and problems before they become critical"). The paradox in these responses is that in this sample the Justice-Rights leaders try to proactively work issues to prevent crisis, but when crisis occurs, they take the sole role in resolving it. The options in question 6 are, (a) "Many decisions a good leader must make by themselves" (the Justice-Rights response) and (b) Involving people in decision-making assures a sense of ownership" (the Care-Connected response).

In the pilot sample, all of the Justice-Rights leaders responded (a) as did 89% of the Dual leaders, and 95% of the Care-Connected leaders. The majority of Dual leaders also selected the Justice-Rights response in question 14 regarding understanding how circumstances versus emotions shape human behavior.

All three leadership groups selected the Care-Connected response in question 15 seeing leadership issues as not clearly all right or all wrong. A strong correlation between the responses of the Dual and Care-Connected leaders exists in question 21, which is concerned with choosing between the needs and the rights of others. Several questions evoked predictable responses with Justice-Rights leaders selecting Justice-Rights responses, Care-Connected leaders selecting Care-Connected responses, and Dual leaders being split evenly between the two options. This occurred on questions 5,8,22, and 23.

The responses to question 27 were quite unexpected. (a) "A moral issue to me would involve my judgments about what is fair and what is right," versus (b) "A moral issue to me would involve my concern about people's feelings and my relationship to them"

When confronted with the direct moral orientation question 100% of the Justice-Rights leaders, 85% of the Dual leaders, and ^^% of the Care-Connected leaders selected the Justice-Rights response. Perhaps this is the expected response for leaders within this business unit.

Quantitative Analysis

Percentage comparisons between moral orientation modes, Justice-Rights (JR), Care-Connected (CC), and Dual (D), and the eight supplemental variables were calculated. These are summarized following each hypothesis statement.

A chi-square test of independence was used to analyze the association of each variable with the moral orientation of the senior leaders. This required combining data so that each cell's expected value was large enough (>5) to make the chi-square statistic accurate. The combined tables are shown at the end of each hypothesis, along with the computed chi-square. For comparison, the chi-square statistics are listed in order of significance in Table 9. For this survey, a strong association is indicated by $p < .05$ and a weak association by $p < .10$. The relatively small number of females in the sample made this statistic less meaningful for the gender variable.

A second set of statistics was calculated to compare the survey variables to the variable of total score (0-27) on the survey. A simple correlation coefficient and its two-tailed significance are shown in Table 10.

Finally, a "one-way" Analysis of Variance (ANOVA) test was accomplished to determine how much of the variation in total score could be explained by differences between subgroups of each survey variable. This holds constant the effects of the other 7 variables to isolate the target variable on variations in total score. An F-ratio statistic was calculated to show the ration of the variance explained between the subgroups versus within the subgroups. The higher the ratio, the better the case for a relationship between the variable and total score. The F- probability restates this statistic in the same terms of significance as discussed above.

In addition, a test for Least Significant Difference (LSD) was performed to see if any of the subgroups could be said to have a mean significantly different from other subgroups at the .05 significance level. This aided in identifying possible non-linear associations between total score and survey variables. These statistics are reposted in Table 11.

H1: Care-Connected moral orientation progressively increases as the age of the leader increases.

Table 1a.
Percentage comparison of Age and Moral Orientation

Moral Orientation	30-39	40-49	50-59	6-+	Participants Response Total
Justice	0	4 (9)	8 (12)	0	12 (9)
Dual	3 (27)	13 (29)	27 (40)	7 (50)	50 (36)
Care	8 (73)	28 (62)	33 (48)	7 (50)	76 (55)
Total	11 (100)	45 (100)	68 (100)	14 (100)	138 (100)

Cell value / (percentage)

In this sample, Dual moral orientation increases with age. Care-Connected moral orientation decrease with age from 30 to 60, then levels off. Justice-Rights orientation showed no apparent trend. The 30 to 39 category and the 60+ groupings had zero Justice-Rights leaders.

In the Leadership sample, when the data are grouped into two Moral Orientation modalities, there is a slight tendency for older leaders to be less Care-Connected. This may be influenced by the fact that males in the sample are significantly older than the females on average. However, the -.079 correlation between age and total moral orientation score (see Table 10) is not significant. When all other variables are held constant through ANOVA testing (see Table 11) there is no significant relationship between age and moral orientation. Both of these sets of statistics lead to a clear rejection of the first hypothesis.

Table 1b.
Combined Age and Moral Orientation

Moral Orientation	30-49	50-59	60+	Total
Justice-Rights (JR) and Dual	20%	35%	7%	62%
Care-Centered	36%	33%	7%	76%
Total20%	56%	68%	14%	138%

Chi-square	DF	p	Min Expected Frequency (MEF)
3.24	2	.198	6.29

H2: Leaders with more education are less Care-Connected than leaders with less education.

Table 2a.
Percentage Comparison of Education and Moral Orientation

Moral Orientation	None	Bachelors	Masters	Doctorate	Participants Response Total
Justice	0	5 (8)	7 (10)	0	12 (9)
Dual	1 (50)	16 (29)	26 (39)	7 (55)	50 (36)
Care	1 (50)	35 (63)	34 (51)	6 (46)	76 (55)
Total	2 (100)	56(100)	67 (100)	13 (100)	138 (100)

Cell value / (percentage)

Thirty-nine percent of masters' degree recipients and 54% of leaders with doctoral degrees scored in the Dual moral orientation range on the Moral Orientation Survey. This means fewer Care-Connected responses given by doctoral degree holders. Sixty-three percent of the bachelors, 51% of the masters, and 46^ of the doctorate leaders were categorized as in the Care-Connected range. This reflects a gradual reduction in the number of Cared-Connected leaders as the level of education increases.

In Table 2b, **Combined Moral Orientation and Education**, education does not appear to be an indicator of higher stages of moral orientation as the chi-square is not statistically significant. Only the negative correlation (-.111 with .197 significance, See Table 10) of degree with total score gives any support to this hypothesis, but it is not statistically significant either. If one also considers the fact that non-Anglos, who tend to be more Care-Connected, have less education than Anglos in this sample, it is easy to see why the ANOVA (Table 11) analysis shows no effect of Education (degree) on one's Total Score on the MOS. The second hypothesis is rejected.

Table 2b.
Combined Moral Orientation and Education

Moral Orientation	Bachelors or less	Masters	Doctorate	Total
Justice-Rights (JR) and Dual	22	33	7	62
Care-Centered	36	34	6	76
Total20%	58	67	13	138

Chi-square	DF	p	Min Expected Frequency (MEF)
2.07	-2	.355	5.84

H3: Anglo leaders are less Care-Connected than non-Anglo leaders.

Table 3a.
Percentage Comparison of Ethnicity and Moral Orientation

Moral Orientation	Non-Anglo	Anglo	Participant Response Total
Justice-Rights	0	7 (6)	7 (5)
Dual	6 (33)	66 (55)	72 (52)
Care-Connected	12 (67)	47 (39)	59 (43)
Total	18 (100)	120 (100)	138 (100)

Cell value / (percentage)

All of the leaders with Justice-Rights moral orientation are Anglo. However, this represents only 5% of the total survey sample. Thirteen percent of the leaders are non-Anglo. One-third of the non-Anglo leaders were categorized as in the Dual moral orientation category. The remaining in two-thirds are categorized as Care-Connected in their moral orientation.

Eighty-seven percent of the sample is Anglo. Fifty-five percent of the Anglos were Dual moral orientation. All non-Anglos were less Justice-Rights oriented than their Anglo counterparts.

Anglos responded with fewer Care-Connected responses than the non-Anglo leaders. The Hispanic leaders were all Care-Connected in their moral orientations. The African American leaders were evenly split between Dual moral orientation and Care-Connected moral orientation. Table 3b, Combined Moral Orientation and Ethnicity, shows moral orientations independent of ethnicity, since the chi-square does not approach statistical significance. However, Table 10, Correlation of Total Score with Survey Variables, and Table 11, Analysis of Variance of Total Score by Survey Variable, show ethnicity approaching statistical significance as a prediction of total score on the Moral Orientation Survey. Reject the 3rd hypothesis.

Table 3b.
Combined Moral Orientation and Ethnicity

Moral Orientation	Non-Anglo	Anglo	Participant Response Total
Justice-Rights and Dual	6	56	62
Care-Connected	12	64	76
Total	18	120	138

Chi-square	DF	p	Min Expected Frequency (MEF)
-1.12	-1	-.289	-8.08

H4: Male leaders are less Care-Connected than female leaders

Table 4a.
Percentage Comparison of Gender and Moral Orientation

Moral Orientation	Female	Male	Participant Response Total
Justice-Rights	0	12 (10)	12 (5)
Dual	2 (22)	48 (37)	50 (36)
Care-Connected	7 (78)	69 (53)	76 (55)
Total	9 (100)	129 (100)	138 (100)

Cell value / (percentage)

Close to 10% of the male respondents were categorized Justice-Rights. Thirty-six percent of the leaders were Dual in their moral orientation. Thirty-seven percent of the male leaders and 22% of the female leaders compose the Dual moral orientation category. Seventy-eight percent of females responded in the Care-Connected range, compared with 53% of the males.

Table 4b.
Combined Moral Orientation and Gender

Moral Orientation	Female	Male	Total
Justice-Rights and Dual	2	60	62
Care-Connected	7	69	76
Total	9		138

Chi-square	DF	p	Min Expected Frequency (MEF)
2.01	-1	-.157	-4.04

The chi-square (see Table 4b) is inappropriate given the low number of females in the sample limiting the minimum expected frequency to <5. On the other hand, the .173 correlation between gender and total moral orientation score is the only correlation that is significant at the .05 level (see Table 10) among the survey variables. This significance is also present using ANOVA (see Table 11). Gender is strongly related to Total Score on the survey. The 4th hypothesis is supported.

H5: Leaders with multiple employer work experience are more Care-Connected than leaders with single employer experiences.

Table 5a.
Percentage Comparison of Other Employers and Moral Orientation

Moral Orientation	One	Two	Three	Four or >	Participant Response Total
Justice-Rights	7 (12)	2 (6)	1 (4)	2 (8)	12 (9)
Dual	20 (35)	15 (43)	6 (29	9 (38)	50 (36)
Care-Connected	31 (53)	18 (51)	14 (67)	13 (54)	76 (55)
Total	58 (100)	35 (100)	21 (100)	24 (100)	138 (100)

Cell value / (percentage)

The largest category in this analysis is composed of leaders who have only worked at this corporation (42%). The largest percentage of Care-Connected workers occurred among those who had worked at three different employers. Forty-three percent of those reporting two employers were Dual orientation. In the Justice-Rights category the largest variable percentage is in the one employer variable (12%). The data do not support any relationship between Moral Orientation and the number of employers as evident in Table 5b (chi-square = 1.40; p =.706), Table 10 (correlation =.037; p = .667, and Table 11 (F-ratio =.21; F-probability =.932).

Table 5b.
Combined Moral Orientation and Number of Employers

Moral Orientation	One	Two	Three	Four or >	Participant Response Total
Justice-Rights and Dual	27	17	7	11	62
Care-Connected	31	18	14	13)	76
Total	58	35	21	24	138

Chi-square	DF	p	Min Expected Frequency (MEF)
1.40	3	.706	9.44

H6: Leaders with work experience at multiple business units are more Care-Connected than leaders with single business unit work experiences.

Table 6a.
Percentage Comparison of the Number of Business Groups and Moral Orientation

Moral Orientation	One	Two	Three	Four or >	Participant Response Total
Justice-Rights	7 (8)	2 (10)	1 (5)	2 (10)	12 (9)
Dual	25 (30)	12 (60)	5 (38)	8 (38)	50 (36)
Care-Connected	51 (62)	6 (30)	8 (57)	11 (52)	76 (55)
Total	83 (100)	20 (100)	14 (100)	21 (100)	138 (100)

Cell value / (percentage)

Leaders who have experiences only with this one particular business unit within this corporation are somewhat more likely to be Care-Connected (62%) particularly compared with those who worked in two groups.

Number of Groups is related to moral orientation but there is a striking nonlinearity in the data. Individuals who have worked in two groups at this corporation have a significantly lower total (are less Care-Connected) score than those who have spent their entire careers in the same group. Table 6b, Combined Moral Orientation (Justice-Rights and Dual versus Care Connected) is dependent on the number of groups at the .10 significance level. This does not hold for those in three or more groups. In the ANOVA (Table 11), the variable approaches significant (p=.106) when other variables are held constant. But the correlation coefficient of -.127 (Table 10) is significant, due to the nonlinearity of the relationship. The 6th hypothesis required linearity to be accepted. The 6th hypothesis is rejected.

Table 6b.
Combined Moral Orientation and Number of Business Groups

Moral Orientation	One	Two	Three	Four or >	Total
Justice-Rights and Dual	32	14	6	10	62
Care- Connected	51	6	8	11	76
Total	83	20	14	21	138

Chi-square	DF	p	Min Expected Frequency (MEF)
-6.53	-3	-.089	-6.29

H7: Leaders with more years at this Fortune 100 Corporation are more Care-Connected.

Table 7a.
Percentage Comparison of the Number of Years at this Corporation and Moral Orientation

Moral Orientation	< 2	3-5	5-10	>10	Participant Response Total
Justice-Rights	1 (14)	0	2 (14)	9 (10)	12 (9)
Dual	0	1 (20)	4 (29)	45 (40)	50 (36)
Care-Connected	6 (86)	4 (80)	8 (57)	58 (52)	76 (55)
Total	7(100)	5 (100)	14 (100)	112 (100)	138 (100)

Cell value / (percentage)

There is a slight tendency for individuals with more years at this company to be less Care-connected. When the data are grouped into Moral Orientation modalities, the relationship is not significant as shown by the chi-square statistics below. The level of significance may be influenced by the non-Anglo sample having fewer years at this corporation, thus reinforcing the tendency. This variable did not show any relationship to Total Score, particularly when other variables are held constant. The 7th hypothesis is rejected.

Table 7b.
Combined Moral Orientation and Number of Years at this Corporation

Moral Orientation	< 2	3-5	5-10	>10	Total
Justice-Rights and Dual	1	1	6	54	62
Care- Connected	6	4	8	58	76
Total	7	5	14	112	138

Chi-square	DF	p	Min Expected Frequency (MEF)
4.37	2	.112	-5.39

H8: Leaders with more years in management are more Care-Connected in their moral orientation

Table 8a.
Percentage of the Number of years in Management and Moral Orientation

Moral Orientation	<2	3-5	5-10	>10	Participant Response Total
Justice-Rights	0	0	2 (7)	10 (11)	12 (9)
Dual	2 (29)	2 (40)	12 (40)	34 (35)	50 (36)
Care-Connected	5 (71)	3 (60)	16(53)	52 (54)	76 (55)
Total	7(100)	5 (100)	30 (100)	96 (100)	138 (100)

Cell value / (percentage)

All Justice-Rights leaders have at least 5 years in management, while leaders with 2 years or less in management scored the highest percentage of Care-connection (71%) Table 8b shows the strong independence of moral orientation to years in management.

No relationship between years I management and total score is indicated by the sample data, as evidenced by -.087 correlation coefficient (see Table 10), and .93 F-ratio (see Table 11). Reject the 8th hypothesis.

Table 8b.
Combined Moral Orientation and Number of Years in Management

Moral Orientation	< 2	3-5	5-10	>10	Total
Justice-Rights and Dual	2	2	14	44	62
Care-Connected	5	3	16	52	76
Total	7	5	30	96	138

Chi-square	DF	p	Min Expected Frequency (MEF)
.720	2	.698	5.39

Table 9.
Chi-square Test of Independence, Moral Orientation versus Survey Variables

Variable	Chi-Square	DF	Significance	Minimum Expected Frequency	Dependent
Age	3.24	2	.198	6.29	No
Education	2.07	2	.355	5.84	No
Ethnicity	1.12	1	.289	8.08	No
Gender	2.01	1	.157	4.04	No*
Number of Employers	1.40	3	.706	9.44	No
Number of Groups	6.53	3	.089	6.29	Weak
Number of Years at Company	4.39	2	.112	5.39	No
Number of Years in Management	0.72	2	.698	5.39	No

Note: Rows and Columns were combed in order to achieve a minimum expected frequency greater than five, if possible. Justice-Rights and Duala moral orientations were combined due to the small number of Justice-Rights individuals.

*Chi-share is not accurate due to the inability to group data and achieve a minimum expected frequency greater than five.

Table 10.
Correlation of Total Score with Survey Variables

Variable	Coefficient	2-tail Significance	More Care-Connected
Age	-.079	.355	Not Significant
Education	-.111	.197	Less Education
Ethnicity	-.173	.043	Females
Gender	-.135	.115	Non-Anglos
Number of Employers	+.037	.667	Not Significant
Number of Groups	-.127	.138	Fewer Groups
Number of Years at Company	-.089	.295	Not Significant
Number of Years in Management	-.087	.310	Not Significant

Table 11.
Analysis of Variance (ANOVA) of Total Score by Survey Variables

Variable	F-Ratio	F-Probability	LSD Test (.05)
Age	1.10	.354	None
Education	.91	.439	None
Ethnicity	2.52	.115	n/a
Gender	4.17	.043	n/a
Number of Employers	.21	.932	None
Number of Groups	2.07	.106	1 > 2*
Number of Years at Company	.41	.748	None
Number of Years in Management	.93	.426	None

*The mean score for individuals I 1 group is significantly higher than for individuals in 2 groups, but no 3 or 4 groups

Research Comparison

The second research question of this study predicted a higher number of Care-Connected leaders in the college president study than in the industry leaders study. The numbers of Care-Connected and Dual leaders were significantly higher in the industry leaders' responses than in the college president study (see Table 12). This finding did not support the original research question than the industry leaders would be less Care-Connected in their moral orientation than the college president sample.

Table 12.
Moral Orientation Comparison, College Presidents and Industry Leaders

Participant Group	Justice-Rights	Dual	Care-Connected
College Presidents	47% (34)	19% (14)	33% (24)
Industry Leaders	9% (12)	36% (50)	55% (76)

percentage / (cell value)

Chi-square	DF	p	Min Expected Frequency (MEF)
51.4	2	<.005	15.77

A second comparison between the two studies derives from an analysis of the results of gender differences in moral orientation. The women in the industry leaders sample were overwhelmingly Care-Connected in their moral orientation responses. Both the Dual and Care-Connected moral orientation modes were higher in the industrial leader group than the college presidents' sample. This also held true for the men in the industry leaders' sample.

Table 13.
Women's Summary Comparison College Presidents and Industry Leaders

Participant Group	Justice-Rights	Dual	Care-Connected
College Presidents	7% (6)	17% (6)	66% (24)
Industry Leaders	0	22% (2)	78% (7)

percentage / (cell value)

Note: Chi-square not meaningful due to sample sizes in the industrial leadership study.

The Industry Leaders group responded significantly higher in the total number of Care-Connected responses that in did the college presidents. This is reflected in the small number of justice-Rights leaders in the industrial leaders' sample. This is contrary to the second research question which predicted a larger number of Care-Connected leaders in the college presidents' sample than the industry leaders' sample.

None of the women in the industry leaders sample were categorized as Justice-Rights. In the college presidents study there was a 4 to 1 ratio of Care-Connected leaners to either the Justice-Rights or the Dual leaders. They have approximately a 3 to 1 ration between the Care-Connected leaders and the Dual leaders in the study of industrial leader.

Table 14.
Men's Summary Comparison College Presidents and Industry Leaders

Participant Group	Justice-Rights	Dual	Care-Connected
College Presidents	50% (18)	22% (8)	28% (10)
Industry Leaders	9% (12)	37% (48)	54% (66)

percentage / (cell value)

Chi-square	DF	p	Min Expected Frequency (MEF)
47.4	2	<.005	6.67

The industry leaders' trend toward more Care-Connected responses is also reflected in the men's responses. Approximately twice as many men in the industry leader sample scored in the Care-Connected range than in the college president sample. The male college president sample scored significantly higher in the Justice-Rights category.

CHAPTER V: CONCLUSTIONS

This chapter consists of two sections, the summary of the study and recommendations for future study.

Summary Discussion of Study

H1: Care-Connected moral orientation progressively increases as the age of the leader increases

This hypothesis was influenced by Valliant's research (1977). His study suggested a tendency for older men to be more relationship focused than they were as younger men, to shift focus form career toward family and relationship in their 50s. This appears to be supported in this study by the comparison between men ages 30-39 and 40-49. However, the 50-59 age category for the E16 leaders is less Care-Connected. This is contrary to the findings of the Valliant (1977) life span research. This slight decrease in Care-Connection regarding age is also unique to the most senior leadership category in this study.

In this study there was a tendency for older leaders to be less Car-Connected. There was no significant relationship between Total Score and age which leads to the rejection of this hypothesis.

H2: Leaders with more education are less Care-Connected than leaders with less education.

Kohlberg alleged there was a direct correlation between an individual's education level and higher moral development (Kohlberg, 1969). In this research sample, the masters and doctorate level leaders were categorized most often as Dual moral orientation. This would reflect fewer Care-Connected responses being given, but not few enough to move them into the Justice-Rights category. Justice-Rights is the highest stage, (5 or 6), in Kohlberg's model (Kohlberg, 1990). There is no statistical relationship between education levels and moral orientation in this study.

H3: Anglo leaders are less Care-Connected than non-Anglo leaders.

This hypothesis was formulated based on my consulting practice experience over the past 10+ years. Non-Anglo senior managers appeared to be more inclusive in their leadership. There was not direct research in the literature on which to base this hypothesis. There were no Justice-Rights leaders in the non-Anglo group. Overall the data reveal that Anglo leaders may be les Care-Connected than non-Anglo leaders, but the sample is too small to support statistical significance.

H4: Male leaders are less Care-Connected than female leaders

Several studies have been conducted reading this hypothesis. Kohlberg's stage theory (1969) of moral development relegates women to the second level, third stage, based on their responses. Gilligan's studies of young women (1982) revealed a second set of moral orientation responses which differed from but she argued, are not less mature than Kohlberg's men. Women develop identity through connectedness (Erickson, 1968). They do not break away in order to establish independence. In one study, (Lyon, 1988) of professional women's moral orientation, Justice-Rights responses were higher than among non-professionals. Overall women continued to favor Care-Connected considerations in resolving conflict.

Desjardins' study of college presidents was selected for comparison with this study sample. Both studies are focused on senior leaders within an organization, making approximately the same pay with comparable educational levels. The college president study supported Gilligan's research.

Gender was the more clearly salient variable in this study. Male respondents were overall less Care-Connected than the female respondents. The surprising difference in this study is the large number of men who responded to the Dual and Care-Connected moral orientations. This is the first study I have seen where the smallest number of male respondents scored in the Justice-Rights moral orientation. In the other studies noted, the dominant male moral orientation was Justice-Rights. In this study, the dominate female moral orientation was Care-Connected.

H5: Leaders with multiple employer work experience are more Care-Connected than leaders with single employer experiences.

This hypothesis was based on the presumption that leaders with work experience at multiple employers would be more Care-Connected due to their experience of different cultures. Creating an organizational environment for inclusion could be experienced as an outcome of Care-Connected leadership. There was no direct research to support this hypothesis. The data from this study did not support any relationship between moral orientation and the number of employers a leader has worked for.

H6: Leaders with work experience at multiple business units are more Care-Connected than leaders with single business unit work experiences.

Piaget's concept of equilibration, the interaction between a person's physical maturation and social experience (Piaget, 1964), introduces the social experience as an element for development. Based on this corporation's cultural profile, the social experience at work could play an important role in a leader's personal development.

The organizational culture of this Fortune 100 Corporation presents an active attempt to balance Justice-Rights and Care-Connected behavioral expectations for employees. The logical antithesis of these expectations by employees would be leaders who are adept at a Dual moral orientation. Both hypothesis 6 and hypothesis 7 were derived based on this corporation's cultural profiled. Although there were clearly a significant number of responding leaders who scored in the Dual moral orientation and Care-Connected moral ordination, there was no clear link between the number of groups in which a leader had worked and moral orientation.

H7: Leaders with more years at this Fortune 100 Corporation are more Care-Connected.

Leaders with over 10 years of service were slightly less Care-Connected than the leaders with less than 10 years of service. There was no significant link between the number of years leaders had worked at this corporation and their moral orientation. This would be consistent with the findings in hypothesis 1. There was a slight trend for the older leader group to be less Care-Connected and the older leader group also had been in management over 10 years.

H8: Leaders with more years in management are more Care-Connected in their moral orientation

The senior managers I have worked with as a consultant have been very interested in the implementation of team-based cultures. The leadership characteristics for teams has a more supportive focus concerned with relationships, mentoring, and inclusive decision making (Manz & Sims, 1989; Fisher, 1993; Lawler, 1992). In addition, the business unit in this study is composed primarily of knowledge workers. Key components to motivating this group are through relationship and freedom (Von Glinow, 1988; Mohrman, Mohrman, & Worley, 1992). These two factors led to the development of this hypothesis, which was not supported by the sample data.

New Findings Discussion

Why do the results of this study fail to support the hypothesis derived from other research? The lack of support this research data of this study was quite unexpected. The expected outcome of the data was that it would not only support the existing body of research in moral orientation, but that the industry leaders in total would score low in the Care-Connected category.

The employees of this Fortune 100 Corporation have been required to have a minimum of 5 days of training each year since 1989. In reviewing the types of course, seminars, or workshops the leaders of this business unit have taken since 1989, 34% of their logged education time was spend in coursework which focused leader development in the areas of coaching, participative decision-making, and team development. These topics are Care-Connected in terms of leadership behaviors. They focus on leading other through inclusion not independent leader decision-making, which would be a more Justice-Rights approach.

Past research on moral orientation for professionals and leaders occurred between 1986 and 1989. For industry, the past 6 to 8 years have been tumultuous times. Team-based and horizontal organizations have emerged during this time frame, both of which have more Care-Connects moral orientation characteristics than Justice-Rights moral orientation characteristics.

Why are there fewer Justice-Rights leaders in this study than in the college president study? The first potential reason for this unexpected data result could be explained in the 10 year time span between the studies. The college president study was conducted in the mid 1980's which was the beginning of many shifts in corporate American culture such as the quality movement and participative management practices. The 10 years between those studies was filled with significant training, changing management behavior to what would be considered more Care-Connected in involving employees in decision-making. The training records of the industry leadership group shows that 34% of their training hours have been spend in this type of training. Perhaps this education effort is being reflected in this study.

A second potential reason for this shift away from Justice-Rights moral orientation in leadership is the sense of what are politically correct responses to the moral orientation questions. This Fortune 100 Corporation has been on an exponential campaign to value diversity, improve productivity through team-based cultures, and building relationships with customers and suppliers. This behavior has been taught and reinforced through goals and performance management. To respond to questions which do not reinforce the importance of these behaviors leaders would be considered counter-cultural within the business unit of this corporation.

Future Study Recommendations

Leadership moral orientation helps to shape decision-making. To get an accurate perspective on the impact leaders' decision-making style has on employees, colleagues, customers, and the overall organization, the Moral Orientation Survey could be completed by individuals representing these categories. These inputs could potentially narrow the gap or increase the correlation between the leaders' self-perceptions regarding their moral orientation and the behavior which other experience. This could either support the leader's self-perception or point out specifics here the differences and similarities occur.

The correlation between the leaders in this study and the amount of management development training in participative or team oriented management techniques could provide additional insight into the development of increased Care-Connected responses. Training coupled with the comprehensive Moral Orientation Survey completion could potentially link leadership development areas to specific coursework to develop Dual moral orientations. This rounded data collection method could include the leader's peers, subordinates, manager, and possibly mentor.

Expanding the research on the relationship between the number of different groups a leader works and the leader's moral orientation could prove significant. This corporation is about to begin an extensive leadership rotational program for experience broadening. Developmentally for future leaders, rotations could prove to be a paradox between the desires to broaden the leader experience and increase leader focus on relationship and inclusion of employees. Additional business units should be assessed using the MOS to baseline the moral orientation of these leader groups to customize the rotations to ensure additional Dual orientation development.

REFERENCES

Argyrus, C., "Teaching smart people how to learn." Harvard Business Review (Man-June, 1991).

Bass. B. (1983). Organizational decision- making. Richard Irwin, Inc.

Belenky, M.F., Clinchy, B.M., Goldgerger, N.R., & Tarule, J.M. (1986). Women's ways of knowing. Basic Books.

Block, P., (1987). The empowered manager. Jossey –Bass Publishers.

Block, P., (1993). Stewardship. Berrett-Koehler Publishers

Bradford, L. & Raines, C., (1992). Twenty something: Today's new work force. New York: MasterMedia Limited.

Colby, A., Kohlberg., L., Gibbs, J., & Lieberman, M. (1983). "A longitudinal study of moral judgment." Monographs of the Society for Research in Child Development, 48 (Serial No. 200).

Dalton, G.W., Thompson, P.H., & Prince, R.L., "The four stages of professional careers: A new look at performance professionals." Organizational Dynamics. (Summer, 1977).

Desjardins., C., (1989). "Gender issues & community college leadership." AAWCJC Journal.

Desjardins, C., (1994). Leadership and gender in the community college. Managing community and junior colleges, eds. A Hoffman and D. Julius, eds. College and University Personnel Association Press.

Douglas, M., (1986). How institutions think. Syracuse University Press.

Driver, M., (1979). Career concepts and career management in organizations. In Behavioral Problems in Organizations. C. Cooper, Ed. Prentice Hall.

Driver, M., (1981). A technical manual for the river decision style exercise: 10 years of research. Center for Effective Organizations, University of Southern California.

Drucker, P., (1968). The age of discontinuity. Harper & Row Publishers.

Drucker, P., The coming of the new organization. Harvard Business Review. (January-February, 1988).

Drucker, P., (1992). Managing for the future. Truman Tally Books.
Edwards, C.P., (1981). The development of moral reasoning in cross-cultural perspective. In R.H. Munroe, R.L.Munroe, & B.B. Whiting (eds). Handbook of cross-cultural human development. Garland Press.

Erikson, E.H. (1968). Identity: Youth and crisis. Norton.

Eichler, M., (1988). Nonsexist research methods. Unwin Hyman Publishers.

Fisher, K., (1993). Leading self-directed work teams. McGraw-Hill Publishers.

Fiske, S.T., & Taylor, S.E. (1991). Social cognition. McGraw-Hill, Inc.

Fuller, L., The case of the speluncean explorers. Harvard Law Review 62:616-45.

Galbraith, J., (1989). "Technology & global strategies and organizations." Center for Effective Organizations. University of Southern California.

Galbraith, J., (1990). Technology and global strategies and structures. In Managing complexity in high technology organizations. M.A. Von Glinow & S.A. Mohrman, eds. Oxford University Press.

Gilligan, C., (1982). In a different voice. Harvard University Press.

Gilligan, C., (1987). Moral orientation and moral development. In Women and moral theory. E.F. Kittay and D.T. Meyers, eds. Totwa, N.J.: Rowman and Littlefield.

Gilligan, C., Ward, J.V., & Taylor, J.M., (1988). Mapping the moral domain. Harvard University Press. Cambridge, Mass.

Gilligan, C., Lyons, N.P., & Hanmer, T.J., (1990). Making connections. Harvard Univerity Press, Cambridge, Mass.

Gilligan, C., & Brown, L.M., (1992). Meeting at the crossroads. Ballantine Books. New York.

Goodman, P., Sproull, L., & Associates. (1990). Technology and organizations. Jossey_Bass Publishers.

Grey, R.J., & Gelford, P.A., "The people side of productivity: Responding to changing employee values." National Productivity Review. (Summer, 1990).

Guglielmino, P.J., & Guglielmino, L.M., (1988). Self-directed learning in business and industry: An information age imperative. In Self-directed learning: application and theory. H.B. Long & Associates, eds. University of Georgia, Department of Adult Education.

Guglielmino, P.J., & Guglielmino, L.M., (1991). Expanding your readiness for self-directed learning. Organization Design & Development, Inc.

Gunneson, E. (1988). Qualitative methods in management research. Bickley Bromlly, U.K.Chartwell-Bratt Ltd.

Hamel, G., & Prahlad, C.K., "Core Competencies," Harvard Business Review. (May-June, 1990).

Hamel, G., & Prahlad, C.K., "Competing for the future". Harvard Business Review. (July-August, 1994).

Harding, M.E., (1970). The way of all women. Shambhala Productions, Inc., Boston.

Helgesen. S., (1990). The female advantage: Women's ways of leadership. Doubleday Currency Publishers.

Heller, F., & Yukl, G.A., "Participation, managerial decision-making, and situation variables." Organizational Behavior and Human Performance. (1969).

Hirschman, A.,(1970). Exit, voice, and loyalty. Harvard University Press.

Horne, K., (1967). Feminine psychology. W.W. Norton & Company, New York.

Jordan, J.V., Kaplan, A.G., Miller, J.B., Surrey, J.L. (1991). Women's growth in connection. Guilford Press.

Jung, C.G., (1956). Aspects of masculine. Bolingen Foundation, Inc.

Jung, C.G., (1959). Aspects of feminine. Bolingen Foundation, Inc.
Kanter, R., "Collaborative advantage: the art of alliances. Harvard Business Review. (July-August, 1994).

Kaplan, R., & Murdock. L., "Rethinking the corporation: core process design." No.2 The McKinsey Quarterly. (1991).

Katzenbach, J., & Smith, D., (1993). The wisdom of teams. Harvard Business School Press.

Kegan. R., (1982). The evolving self. Harvard University Press.

Kessler-Harris, A., (1981). Women have always worked. The Feminist Press.

Kittay, E.F., & Meyers, D.T., (1987). Women and moral theory. Rowman and Lifflefield Publishers, Inc.

Klein., S.B., (1991). Learning: principles and applications. McGraw-Hill, Inc.

Knowles, M., (1975). Self-directed learning. Association Press.

Kohlberg, L., (1964). Development of moral character and moral ideology. In M.L. Hoffman & L.W. Hoffman (eds). Review of Child Development Research. (Vol.1). Russell Sage.

Kohlberg, L. (1969)., Stage and sequence: The cognitive-developmental approach to socialization. In D. A. Goslin (ed). Handbook of Socialization Theory and Research. Rand McNally.

Kohlberg, L., (1973). "The claim to moral adequacy of a highest stage of moral development." Journal of Philosophy. 70:630-646.

Kohlberg, L., (1976). Moral stages and moralization: The cognitive developmental approach. In T. Liken (ed). Moral Development and Behavior. Holt, Rinehart, and Winston.

Kohlberg, L., (1984). Essay on moral development. Harper & Row Publishers.

Kohlberg, L., & Gilligan, C., (1972) The adolescent as a philosopher: The discover of the self in the postconventional world. In J. Kagan & R. Coles (eds). 12 to 16 Early Adolescent. Norton.

Kotter, J.P., (1990). A force for change: How leadership differs from management. The Free Press.

Langdale. S., (1983). “Moral Orientations and Moral Development: The Analysis of Care and Justice Reasoning across Different Dilemmas in Females and Males rom Childhood through Adulthood.” Doctoral dissertation. Harvard Graduate School of Education.

Lawler, E. (1971). Pay and organizational effectiveness: A psychological view. McGraw-Hill.

Lawler, E., (1984). “The New Pay.” Center for Effective Organizations, University of Southern California.

Lawler, E., Renwick, P., & Bullock, R., “Employee influence on decisions: An analysis.” Center for Effective Organizations. University of Southern California.

Lawler, E. (1992). The ultimate advantage. Jossey-Bass.

Maccoby, M., (1989). Motivating and leading the new generation. Touchstone Books.

Manz, C. C., & Sims, H.P> (1989). Superleadership. Prentice Hall Press.

Manz, C.C. & Sims, H.P., “Superleadership creates a new perspective for managers,” The Journal for Quality and Participation. (June, 1990).

Mantz, C. C., Keating, D. E., & Donnellon, A. “Preparing for an organizational change to employee self-management: The managerial transition,” Organizational Dynamics. (1990).
McGregor, D., (1960). The human side of enterprise. McGraw Hill Publishers.

McKinnon P. "Steady state people: A third career orientation." Research Management. (January-February, 1987).

Melcher, A.J., (1980). Structure and process of organizations: A systems approach. Prentice-Hall, Inc.

Mintzberg, H., (1973). The nature of managerial work. New York: Harper & Row.

Mintzberg, H., (1989). Mintzberg on management. Free Press.

Mohrman, S. A., & Von Glinow, M., "High technology organizations: Context, organization, and people." Journal of Engineering and Technology Management. (November, 1988).

Mohrman, S. A., & Cummings, T.G., (1989). Self-designing organizations: Learning to create high performance. Addison-Wesley.

Mohrman, S., Mohrman,A., & Worley, C, (1992). "Performance management in the highly interdependent world of high technology." Center for Effective Organizations. University of Southern California.

Noddings, N., (1984). Caring: A feminine approach to ethics and moral education. University of California Press.

Nomilos, G., "Managing knowledge workers for productivity." National Productivity Review. (Spring, 1989).

Osburn, J., (1990). Self-directed work teams. Zenger-Miller.
Packer, M.J. (1985). "Hermeneutic inquiry in the study of human conduct." American Psychologist, 43:2 1081-1093.

Papalio, D., & Olds, S., (1992). Human development. (5th ed.) McGraw-Hill, Inc.

Passmore, W.A., (1988). Designing effective organizations: The sociotechnical systems perspective. John Wiley & Sons.

Piaget, J., (1964). Six psychological studies. Vintage Books.

Piaget, J., (1965). The moral judgment of the child. Free Press (Original work published 1932).

Piaget, J., & Inhelder, B., (1969). The psychology of the child. Basic Books.

Piskurch,G., (1993). Self-directed learning. Jossey-Bass.

Rawls, J., (1971). The theory of justice. Harvard University Press, Cambridge.

Rosener, J.B., "Ways women lead." Harvard Business Review. (November-December, 1990).

Rummler, G., & Brache, A., (1990). Improving performance: How to manage the white space on the organization chart. Jossey-Bass.

Schaef, A. W., (1988). The addictive organization. Harper & Row Publishers. San Francisco.

Schein, E.H., "Reassessing the "Divine Rights" of Managers". Sloan Management Review. 63 (Winter, 1989).

Sharpio, G., & Sica,A., (eds). (1984). Hermeneutics: questions and prospects. Amherst, MA: University of Mass Press.

Shrivastave, P., "A typology of organizational learning systems." Journal of Management Studies, (1983).

Smith, M.F., (1991). The moral orientation of school leadership and student achievement: an internal investigation into relationships. Doctoral Dissertation, University of Texas at Austin, University Microfilms International.

Snow, C., Miles, R., & Coleman, H., Jr. "Managing 21st century networked organizations." Organizational Dynamics, (Winter, 1992).

Strata, R., "Organizational learning: The key to management innovation." Sloan Management Review. (Spring, 1989).

Tannenbaum, R., & Schmdt, W. "How to choose a leadership pattern." Harvard Business Review. (1958).

Tarvis, C.,(1992). Mismeasure of woman. Simon & Shuster, New York.

Thomas, R., Jr., (1990). Manage people not personnel. Harvard Business Review.

Torbet, W. (1991). The power of balance. Sage Press.

Vaillant, G.E., (1997). Adaptation to life. Little, Brown Publishers.

Von Glinow, M., (1988). The new professionals: managing today's high-tech employees. Ballinger Publishing Company.

Vroom, V.H., & Yetton, P.W., (1973). Leadership and decision-making. University of Pittsburg Press.

Weick, K., "Organization design: Organizations as self-designing systems." Organizational Dynamics. (Autumn, 1977).

Wheatley, M.J., (1992). Leadership and the new science. Berrett-Koehler, Publishers, Inc.

APPENDIX A
SURVEY COVER LETTER

Date

Dear Senior Manager,

As a member of senior management, you have been selected through a random sample method to participate in a research study.

Enclosed are two documents, the survey instrument and a participant release form. Please complete the enclosed survey and return it in the envelop marked "Survey Return". It should take you approximately 30 minute to complete the survey.

You may be assured of complete confidentiality. The questionnaire has an identification number for blind check off purposes. Your survey responses will be tabulated by a third party statistician not attached to _____(Name of Corporation_____ . Your name will never be placed on the questionnaire. The results will be available to anyone other than in summary form.

The results of this research will not directly use the corporation's name. It will be referred to as a for-profit Fortune 100 Corporation.

The participant release form must be signed and returned in the envelop maker "Release Form Return". To insure the anonymity of your response, please **DO NOT** return both the survey instrument and the participant release form I the same envelop.

I will be most happy to answer any questions you might have. Please write or call.

Thank you for your assistance,
Sincerely,

Susan Harwood

APPENDIX B
MORAL ORIENTATION SURVEY
(Sample questions)

INSTRUCTIONS: Each question consists of two statements. Circle the letter of the statements in each question which best describes you. If both statements are accurate in describing your approach, circle the statement which you would do first. Circle only one letter per number.

1. A. I focus on the outcomes of decision making, rather than the process.
   B. I focus on the process of decision making rather than the outcomes.

2. A. I take peoples' feelings and needs into account in making decisions.
   B. I take budget and institutional issues into account in making decisions.

3. A. I work hard to insure that people know what I expect of them.
   B. I work hard to have people feel that they are being heard.

SUPPLEMENTAL DATA FORM

INSTRUCTIONS: Please circle the number as appropriate.

1. Your Age:	5. Your Degrees Earned:
3.1 Under 30 3.2 30-39 3.3 40-49 3.4 50-59 3.5 60+	5.1 None 5.2 Bachelors 5.3 Masters 5.4 Doctorate
2. Your Gender:	6. Your Ethnicity:
2.1 Female 2.2 Male	6.1 African American 6.2 Anglo 6.3 Asian American 6.4 Hispanic 6.5 Native American 6.6 Other
3. Your Number of Years as a Manager:	7. Your Number of Years at this Corporation
3.1 2 years or less 3.2 3-5 years 3.3 5-10 years 3.4 over 10 years	7.1 2 years or less 7.2 3-5 years 7.3 5-10 years 7.4 over 10 years
4. Number of different Groups (of this Corporation)you have worked in:	8. How many other employers have your worked for in your career other than this corporation?
4.1 1 4.2 2 4.3 3 4.4 4 or more	8.1 1 8.2 2 8.3 3 8.4 4 or more

APPENDIX C
PARTICIPANT FEEDBACK LETTER

Date
Name and address of participant

Dear XXXXXXX

Thank you for completing and returning the leadership study survey. As promised, enclosed are the results of the entire study on leadership orientations of senior managers at a for-profit Fortune 100 corporation.

The sample population consisted of ***E13, ***E14, ***E15, and ***vice presidents. The responses were divided into three categories: Care-Centered; Justice Rights, and Balance (Dual).

The purpose of this study was twofold. First, to assess the moral orientation of the officer core at a large for-profit corporation, these findings will be compared to comparable studies conducted with college presidents.

Secondly, the more we understand about successful leaders within successful corporations, the better we can select and mentor emerging leaders.

If you have further questions regarding this study or comparable studies conducted, please feel free to contact me.

Again, thank you for your participation

Sincerely yours,

Susan Harwood
Address / phone

WALKER PUBLICATIONS

Walker Publications specializes in unique innovative writers with unique approaches to topics. Novice and experienced authors find the Walker process simple with a responsive staff to assist in the journey of publishing.

Poised at the leading edge of the "*New Way to Conduct Business*", Walker writers blend mind, body, and spirit in the essence of their writing to deliver holistic relevant works for individuals, groups, and organizations.

.

Walker Publications
E: ideas@walkerpublications.co
W: www.walkerpublications.co

www.ingramcontent.com/pod-product-compliance
Lightning Source LLC
Chambersburg PA
CBHW060906280326
41934CB00007B/1204

* 9 7 8 0 9 8 8 2 5 0 8 1 9 *